The Art of the
NATIVE
AMERICAN
FLUTE

The Art of the
NATIVE AMERICAN FLUTE

by

R. Carlos Nakai *and* James DeMars

with additional material by
David P. McAllester
Ken Light

CANYON RECORDS PRODUCTIONS
PHOENIX · ARIZONA

Edited by Robert and Giuli Doyle.
Book design by Larry Lindahl Design.
Photography by John Running.
Illustration by Larry Lindahl.
Music copy by Joel DiBartolo.

Published by Canyon Records,
3131 West Clarendon Avenue, Phoenix,
Arizona 85017, telephone (800) 268-1141.
Canyon Records is a subsidiary of the
Doyle Music Group, Inc.
Please Visit Us:
www.CanyonRecords.com
www.NativeAmericanMusicNews.com
www.NativeAmericanMusicPodcasts.com

facebook.
Join Canyon Records' Facebook at:
Facebook.com/CanyonRecords

Follow us at:
twitter
Twitter.com/CanyonRecords
myspace.com
a place for music
MySpace.com/CanyonRecords

Material in Part I, Chapter 2, is used with
permission from Ken Light, Amon Olorin Flutes,
492 Lemlama Lane, Arlee, Montana 59821,
telephone (406) 726-3353.
www.AOflutes.com

The initial version of Part III appeared in
To the Four Corners: A Festschrift in Honor of Rose Brandel
Ellen C. Leichtman, editor
Detroit Monographs in Musicology/Studies in
Music Harmonie Park Press

Celestial Harmonies album covers are reproduced
with permission from Celestial Harmonies,
P.O. Box 30122, Tucson, Arizona 85751, telephone
(520) 326-4400. www.Harmonies.com

Silver Wave album covers are reproduced with
permission from Silver Wave Records, P.O. Box 7943,
Boulder, Colorado 80306, telephone (800) SIL-WAVE.

Manufactured in the U.S.A.

Library of Congress Catalog Card Number: 95-071172
ISBN 978-0-9647886-0-2
ISBN #0-9647-8860-8

CONTENTS

PART III *THE MUSIC OF R. CARLOS NAKAI*

PREFACE

S PRODUCER FOR CANYON RECORDS PRODUCTIONS, I HAVE HAD THE PLEASURE OF WORKING WITH R. CARLOS NAKAI SINCE 1983 WHEN CANYON RELEASED his first album. Through the years we've received requests from his fans and students of the Native American flute for copies of his music. Part II solves that need in part with transcriptions from several of Carlos' albums. Hopefully, the chapters on learning the flute will give beginning students a starting point and experienced players further thoughts to enhance their playing. Two of Carlos' many collaborators assisted with these sections: flute maker Ken Light provided material on the care of the traditional flute and James DeMars, Ph.D., provided material on general music education, editorial assistance and transcriptions of two of his compositions.

We also wanted to create a reference source for those interested in studying Carlos' music and his career. Thus, the inclusion of Part III which features a discussion of Carlos' recordings by the eminent ethnomusicologist David McAllester, Ph.D. We hope this section will give readers a good perspective on the place of this unique artist who bridges, through his performances and recordings, the traditional and mainstream cultures of contemporary America.

ROBERT DOYLE

EDITORS' NOTE: For those who do not read music, we recommend that you begin with Chapter 6, "Standard Notations and Variations," for an overview of European notation.

PART I

THE NATIVE AMERICAN FLUTE

NATIVE AMERICAN MUSICAL TRADITION

THE USE OF THE FLUTE IN THE CULTURES OF THE INDIGENOUS NORTH AMERICAN PEOPLES CAN BE TRACED BACK AT LEAST 2,500 YEARS THROUGH ORAL traditions and ancient pictographs. In the Southwest, depictions of the hump-backed flute player Kokopelli, a minor deity symbolizing travel and change, are found in abandoned pueblos and upon rock faces such as the well-known Newspaper Rock in southern Utah, in the ruins of the ancient Mississippian cultures and in the remains of the Central and South American pre-Columbian cultures.

In the western plains tribes, such as the Sioux, there are legends about the origins and use of the flute:

> *Ya Hominni was sad, he and his brothers were lonely and needing companionship. In his travail he became aware of Hehaka who had many, many female consorts and admirers.*

He consulted Hehaka for advice and assistance in attracting many admirers, too. While in discussions, Pehangila and Siyo sat close by and listened quietly. Soon afterward they called to Hehaka for a private conference. Hehaka advised Ya Hominni to rest for a spell and they would call for him when they had finished their discussions.

Ya Hominni slept and had a profound dream in which Hehaka, Pehangila and Siyo presented four songs and a simple musical instrument that he would use to charm and attract many admirers. They further instructed Ya Hominni in the ways of a society which would be called the Elk Dreamer society that would be imbued with the power of the Bull Elk through the use of the flute.

Thus began the Wiiyape tradition among the Lakota and the society of Ya Hominni Siyo Tanka.

...the flute began to reappear as people of all cultural backgrounds were drawn to its pure, timeless sound.

In the years of official suppression of native culture, the use of the flute was lost by many tribes and continued as a small part of the tribal cultures in which it remained. In the 1970s the use of the flute began to reappear as people of all cultural backgrounds were drawn to its pure, timeless sound. Recordings by such performers as Doc Tate Nevaquaya, Tom Mauchahty Ware and Kevin Locke helped to reintroduce the traditional flute. My own efforts as a performer and composer were met with greater and greater interest including many questions about how to play the flute. People not only wanted to hear this ancient instrument but wanted to play it themselves. And while more flute makers were beginning to craft instruments to meet this demand, a clear methodology for learning or teaching Native American flute performance was lacking.

Reliable historical documentation, culturally specific teachings and knowledge about the traditions of flute-making, performance and philosophy were largely non-existent. Colonization, government suppression and overt cultural change forced many tribes to abandon significant portions of their oral traditions, both sacred and social, in order to survive in a quickly changing and oft-times hostile world.

The nature of the flute itself also provided problems in developing teaching and learning techniques. Made by craftpersons of varied tribal backgrounds these individually-crafted instruments each have its own idiosyncrasies (each is unique depending upon choices of the individual maker). Many problems of discerning pitch, pitch range, fingering patterns, embouchure, etc., beset me as I attempted to develop a technique that would adequately serve me in playing any Native American flute by any maker. The arbitrary methods for crafting the traditional flute encouraged me to come up with a method to help understand the unique aspects of its sound production.

The arbitrary and distinctive nature of each of these closely related instruments encouraged more research and my personal involvement as a composer and performing artist began with much interviewing, experimentation and personal observations of a number of flute makers and players. I found that the burgeoning variety of home-made tablature systems for specific kinds of Native American flutes did not coherently address a single method that could be used successfully with a wide variety of flutes, regardless of their ethnic origins. As I became more involved with producing written notation related to the varied pitch ranges and fingering techniques for each instrument, the need for a consistent written method became more and more apparent.

Additionally, keeping separate and distinct manuscripts for each Native American flute in my performance collection quickly resulted in a confusing pile of paper notations. Memorizing and remembering what each flute could perform became a rather unwieldy task. The European system of transposition did not work in any case, to say the least, as these instruments do not play in the European diatonic system.

Needless to say, my early flute days included a fair amount of consternation and frustration in having to memorize a number of separate and seemingly unrelated finger patterns and scales. In fact, I accepted the mistaken assumption that these instruments, quite possibly, were not made correctly and therefore could not perform correctly. I was faced with the question, "What is the right way?"

Out of my initial frustration, I discovered that the Native American flute is an excellent teaching device. The flute forced me to confront my heretofore highly idealized self and the farce of enforcing strict conformity and inflexible rules (perhaps I'd been infected with the same colonial attitude that confused early ethnographers in their attempts to legitimize the wide spectrum of indigenous native music in North America and elsewhere).

Hence, I began to organize and originate this method for understanding the limitations and versatility of a uniquely crafted and arbitrarily-keyed sound sculpture that shares its basic configuration with the most primitive and most technically developed flutes throughout the world (interestingly, I found that the "primitive" technology of the cedar flute is essentially the same technology used on a much larger scale in that elaborate collection of flutes we call the pipe organ).

The flute forced me to confront my heretofore highly idealized self and the farce of enforcing strict conformity and inflexible rules.

In developing this methodology I explored recordings by Doc Tate Nevaquaya (*Comanche Flute Music*, Ethnic Folkways Records, FE-4328), Tom Mauchahty Ware (*Flute Songs of the Kiowa and Comanche*, Indian House, IH-2512 and *The Traditional and Contemporary Indian Flute of the Kiowa-Comanche*, Indian Sounds, IS-5050) and Kevin Locke (*Lakota Love Songs and Stories: Lakota Wiikijo Olowan*, Featherstone, FS-4001). Each recording contained valuable information about the Native American flute from the tribal perspectives of each of the players. A thesis by Ed Wapp, available by interlibrary loan from the University of Washington in Seattle, provided information about the central plains and woodlands flute of the Sioux people.

As part of my research I studied existing sources of performance technique for the European silver flute such as the *Rubank Elementary Method* by A.C. Peterson and *Pares Scales for Flute* by Gabriel Pares. Another reliable source that was "flute specific" in regard to the European tradition, *The Flute* by Philip Bate, Instruments of the Orchestra (Benn and Norton), provided information about flute craftsmanship, aerodynamics of sound production, performance technique and historical resource information.

And so, through research, experimentation, personal experience and trial and error, I developed the methodology before you. It is designed to simplify, for both the experienced player and the beginner, the mysteries of performing one of the most evocative and expressive instruments in the world...the Native American flute.

NATIVE AMERICAN MUSICAL STYLES

Music is a vital tradition in the sacred and social worlds of native North American peoples. In day to day life, music provides more than simple pleasure and entertainment and also serves to preserve, especially through song, the integrity of experience based oral traditions. The individuals, often ceremonial singers, who personalize and interpret the spiritual and philosophic lifeways use music as a foundation to reinforce cultural concepts. A study of indigenous native music requires adequate knowledge and understanding of tribal variations in language, oral histories, religious and healing practices and music traditions. The traditions are always changing as acculturation and adaptation bring new songs and stories to each generation.

Tribal communities have each originated unique styles of solo and accompanied vocal music that can use a wide variety of percussion

...one of the most evocative and expressive instruments in the world... the Native American flute.

instruments. The music is largely functional with the particulars of the performance affecting the choice of songs and their structure. The purposes of the event may be reflected in a particular use of meaningful words and phrases. And yet, use of phonetic vocables may allow the performers to include, for pleasure in a social setting, musical material from sacred ceremonies and rituals that "just sound good." Essentially, three general areas of traditional music can be distinguished as follows:

Sacred, Ceremonial and Ritual Music

This most traditional form of indigenous music is dictated by the centuries of practitioners who dutifully instructed novices in the proper etiquette and unvaried recollection of significant songs. Creation and emergence chants, ceremonial and ritual songs that express community expectations through rites of passage, healing songs derived from ancient historic chants gives continuity to the lives of the people. These songs are the historic link to past experience expressed as the developing mythology of a culture.

Sacred and ceremonial songs are usually performed by a solo chanter or by small groups of similarly trained vocalists accompanied by a variety of percussion instruments. In many instances, this kind of music is performed in strictly defined duple meter patterns. Extra beats and syncopated rhythm patterns are carefully orchestrated to accentuate changes in the meter, cadence or in the overall style of the song. Tempo and dynamics are determined by the use and manner of presentation. Text or vocalized portions are usually repeated a number of times in various sequences to include all or significant sections of epic tales in prose form. Occasionally, descriptive percussion patterns and particular song stylizations will augment visual expressions of particular activities to add interest.

Since many tribes have limited means to store and retrieve their extensive histories and traditions, they rely heavily upon song, story and dance to codify and record their historic traditions for future generations. Thus, this creates the need to structure intricately worded tales upon simply organized patterns of vocal and percussion accompaniment, like lyrics in modern music. In the close-knit kinship system of most tribal peoples, their holistic philosophy encourages individuality and freedom of expression built upon the rich foundation of oral tradition, spirituality and philosophies. The historic basis of these songs serves as a road map for understanding and living in the present day world and may guide individuals in their life journeys.

…to store and retrieve their extensive histories and traditions, they rely heavily upon song, story and dance…

Social and Secular Songs

These songs are derived from various sources to add ambiance to community wide ritual activities and rites of passage. Also, the social music category is not a clear cut genre but overlaps the sacred and personal forms. While sacred and ceremonial songs make up a major part of the music of native peoples, social music occupies an important niche in the daily activities of the community. Here, the stringent demands of strict form, meter and tempo of sacred songs are relaxed a bit. Most social songs are easy to listen to or will encourage listeners to actively participate. Social music may have stylistic variations in language, in dialect or manner of pronunciation with the accompaniment occasionally including more voices and more varied percussion.

Personal and Improvisational Music

This music is quite variable and expressive and uses the full range of music options available to the individual composer/arranger. This expression is derived from sacred and social contexts and may remind the listener of spiritual pathways or detail significant occurrences in one's life. Aficionados of this rich indigenous personal music are often inspired by its freshness and hard to describe spiritual quality or they respond to the impressionistic artistry that reflects cross-cultural influences. These personal and interpersonal expressions easily demonstrate the adaptability of traditional culture to change and to the need to adjust to the varied demands of life in a multi-cultural society of other human beings.

...social music occupies an important niche in the daily activities of the community.

2

THE NATIVE AMERICAN FLUTE

THE NATIVE AMERICAN FLUTE IS AN END-BLOWN VERTICALLY HELD BLOCK FLUTE, BELONGING TO THE FAMILY OF INSTRUMENTS CALLED FLUTE-A-BEC, THAT USES a movable flue, diaphragm and a chimneyed air-directing apparatus to produce sound. Manipulation of these pieces enables a degree of control over the brilliance of pitch throughout the extended scale and will affect the frequency of the distinctive warble sound common to well-made traditional instruments when all finger positions are closed.

Actual pitch ranges and tonal quality are determined by the internal bore size, the length of the working portion of the pipe body/variable tube, the finger hole distances and the sound-producing mechanism position. The variety of construction techniques by various flute makers accounts for a diversity of sound quality and and a chimneyed air-directing apparatus to produce sound. Manipulation of these pieces enables a degree of control over the brilliance of pitch throughout the extended scale and will affect the frequency of the distinctive warble sound common to well-made traditional instruments in the all-closed finger position.

Actual pitch ranges and tonal quality are determined by the internal bore size, the length of the working portion of the pipe body/variable tube, the finger hole distances and the sound-producing mechanism position. The variety of construction techniques by various flute makers accounts for a diversity of sound quality and often typifies sounds belonging to specific tribal groups. Variations in the materials used in the body stock, which range from juniper, ironwood, ebony, pine to cedar, have a marked effect upon the resonance and clarity of the flute's extended scale range.

The Native American flute has three working parts that are hand carved into two halves of a split tube. These halves are glued together and secured by various means to keep them aligned and air-tight. This insures that the sound-producing dynamics of air movement over a block and against an edge is as efficient as possible. In fact, I have found that even using modern tools and processes in crafting the instruments one must frequently use trial and error to arrive at the best method for making the flute work effectively.

The anterior end of the flute is comprised of the mouthpiece/mouthpipe opening directly connected to the *air chamber* (Figure 1). The chamber and flue design creates an internal back-pressure that allows the instrumentalist to control the intensity of air released through the shallow and narrow slot carved into the top of the block (or created with the addition of a spacer plate over the block), called the *flue*. The flue is partially overlaid with a flat-bottomed cover called the *bird* or *saddle*. The bird or saddle effectively directs the air stream more upward or downward against a thin *edge* of metal, fiber, wood or other found item or the distal edge of the spacer plate. In many cases, a well-made Native American flute can be played like a transverse flute by blowing against an edge of the hole. At this juncture the Native American flute works like any other basic flute.

On the distal end, the *variable tube* is pierced by one to six regularly spaced finger holes that lengthen or shorten the tube, depending upon what holes or combination of holes are covered, to produce higher or lower sounding pitches. In the manual, *The Flutist's Progress,* by Walfrid Kujala and in a *Scientific American* article entitled "The Physics of the Pipe Organ," the harmonics of sound production directly relating to the Native American flute are discussed. A standing sine wave pattern vibrates in a air column within the variable tube. The column is shortened or lengthened by opening

The variety of construction techniques by various flute makers accounts for a diversity of sound quality and often typifies sounds belonging to specific tribal groups.

FIGURE 1. Components of the Native American Flute

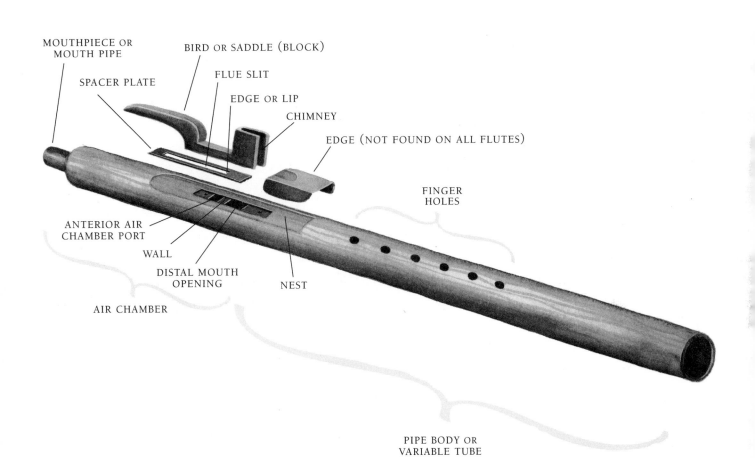

MOUTHPIECE OR
MOUTH PIPE

BIRD OR SADDLE (BLOCK)

SPACER PLATE

FLUE SLIT

EDGE OR LIP

CHIMNEY

EDGE (NOT FOUND ON ALL FLUTES)

FINGER
HOLES

ANTERIOR AIR
CHAMBER PORT

WALL

DISTAL MOUTH
OPENING

NEST

AIR CHAMBER

PIPE BODY OR
VARIABLE TUBE

or closing the finger holes in various combinations to increase or decrease the rate of vibration of the standing wave that creates a fundamental tone and harmonic series. Mr. Kujala states:

> *All musical tones are complex combinations of harmonic*
> *sounds. The number and relative strength of these harmonics are,*
> *in fact, what determine the color and timbre of the musical sound,*
> *giving the clarinet, the oboe, the bassoon, the violin, the flute,*
> *or any other instrument their characteristic identifying qualities.*
> *In addition, the player, by imaginative control of breath and*
> *embouchure, puts his (her) own stamp on the harmonic structure*
> *of his (her) flute sound, determining the more subtle qualities of*
> *tone, whether it is to be sweet or coarse, brilliant or mellow, breathy*
> *or focused, light or dark.*

...each flute [is]

a personally

crafted and

arbitrarily keyed

instrument.

Personalizing these tones through breath control and embouchure (positioning of the lips) techniques helps to aurally distinguish one flute player's sound from another. Certain figures and styles of accents that embellish notes, passages and phrases also adds to the personalization of Native American flute sounds.

Flute lengths vary in a range from roughly twelve to fifty-five centimeters. The placement of the sound-producing apparatus as well as the finger hole distances are arbitrarily determined. Measurements for distances are derived from the maker's own body. For instance, combinations of arm length with or without palm and/or finger length, the width or length of the hand, thumb width, digit width or lengths of any other fingers of the hand contribute to the template of each flute maker thereby making each flute a personally crafted and arbitrarily keyed instrument.

The visual conformation of the Native American flute is divided into quarters of the overall length. It is placement of the working parts relative to the overall shape that gives the flute the balanced feel and appearance of a sculptural artwork rather than a decidedly technical instrument.

The mouthpiece end including the air chamber is roughly one-fourth the total length (see Figure 1). The block placement and sound-producing mechanism falls within this area but is less than one-half the total length of the flute. The distance of the first finger hole, that which is closest to the sound-producing mechanism, is roughly one-eighth the distance to the next quarter or the half-way mark of the whole instrument (measured by one palm width from the center of the block). Other finger hole spacings are roughly a thumb's width or the digit between the second and third joints of the pointer finger. Upon reaching the three-quarters distance of the variable tube, the extreme end is roughly determined, regardless of finger hole placement, by the width of the palm plus or minus a finger or thumb width and marks the cutoff point, carved effigy placement or tuning hole position at the end of the instrument. For this reason, no two flutes work exactly alike, even those made by the same maker.

The technique of sound production is relatively easy and is essentially the same as the other end-blown flutes. Gently but deliberately blow air through the mouthpiece, supporting your breath with your diaphragm. For an idea of the proper way to hold the flute in your lips, see Figure 3 and the cover of this book. Don't be frustrated, if at first, your tone is breathy or uncontrolled. It may take awhile before you develop your wind and discover how much air pressure it will take to make a pleasing tone. However, unique variations in the following areas (which will be addressed in following chapters) require practice and the development of technical skill to create the typically soothing sound of the Native American flute:

- limited pitch range
- the basic scale and extended scale
- breath control and phrasing
- tones not found in contemporary tuning
- idiomatic ornaments and cadences
- parlando rhythms

...no two flutes work exactly alike, even those made by the same maker.

CARE AND MAINTENANCE

Any condition that affects the flow of air in the flute will affect the sound producing mechanism and cause a loss of tone. The most common problem of this sort is caused by condensation of water droplets in the flue. Anytime warm, moist air (such as your breath) contacts a colder surface, condensation will occur. Drops of water can form in the flue and get in the way of the air flow effectively squeezing off the flute's tone. This is called "watering out" and is common to all wind instruments. While keeping the flute warm will help avoid condensation, you will need to know how to properly dry out your flute.

When "watering out" does occur shaking out or swinging the flute while firmly grasping the variable tube end will clear the collected moisture from the flue. Sucking air back through the flue or holding a finger in front of the saddle chimney and blowing air without producing a tone helps to collect moisture in the air chamber or even blow it out entirely. If time permits, completely disassemble the saddle-space-block mechanism and thoroughly dry using a cotton swab and set aside for later assembly. This is the most efficient drying method and will prevent cracking of the flute body or swelling of the sound producing parts.

Conscientious care and maintenance after extended playing should include complete disassembly, drying and lightly oiling the surfaces that frequently become wet, such as the bottom of the saddle, the top and air chamber side of the block and the surfaces contacted by the spacer-plate. If these parts become moisture damaged, the flute must be revoiced by the maker which involves refitting the block, spacer-plate and nest to prevent air from leaking out the sides of the sound-producing apparatus. Heated drying with hair dryers, paint removers or other hot air appliances will increase the possibility of warping and formation of leaks.

Wiping the exterior of the flute with a good quality paste-type furniture wax will retain the finish and beauty of the wood. On my flutes I use an all-natural finish of linseed oil and beeswax that may require periodic rewaxing.

The cedar flute is relatively fragile and must be protected from physical damage.

A sturdy, crush-proof case is a necessity and one can be constructed, at minimum expense, from a tube of PVC with ends caps and sufficient foam. Be careful to not let your flute become the plaything of your pets. Dogs particularly enjoy the flavor of the smoked buckskin wrap that holds the block in place and can continue from there with devastating results.

The Native American flute is a relatively non-fussy instrument that requires little maintenance. Protect it from accidental damage, deal with moisture condensation, maintain the exterior finish and it will provide you with a lifetime of playing enjoyment.

The cedar flute is relatively fragile and must be protected from physical damage.

3

Tunings and Finger Patterns

N RESEARCHING VARIATIONS
IN THE PITCHES OF TRADITIONALLY CRAFTED FIVE AND SIX FINGER-
HOLE NATIVE AMERICAN FLUTES, I HAVE FOUND GENERAL PITCH
and key relationships. Flutes from the woodland regions commonly sound
within a diatonic major scale range comparable to E and flutes from the
central and southern plains to B-flat. Further, I compared the basic performance pitches, eight in all, as being closely related to the pitches of the
harmonic/melodic minor key ranges of B-minor, C-minor, F-sharp minor
and G-minor respectively. Although each individually crafted instrument
has similarities within their pitch ranges the starting and ending notes vary
considerably. Pitch separations by whole and half steps and the location of
unplayable pitches within the range of each Native American flute become
evident using standard basic flute fingering techniques. I have termed this
an arbitrarily keyed system of flute design (I have not found any system that
works in the early ethnographic whole or five-toned scale). Instead, it

appears that the natural scale of each traditionally crafted Native American flute is directly related to the vocal music performed within the maker's tribal culture and is totally outside the diatonic (whole, whole, half-step, whole, whole, whole, half-step) system of European diatonic major scales.

However, as in Amon Olorin flutes and others of historic and contemporary manufacture, I have correlated most to the modes related to the E, B, B-flat, and F-major scales. Consequently, the lydian, mixolydian, dorian and phrygian modes of these major scales can be used to typify the step arrangement of the eight basic pitches of the Native American flute in the European system.

Every major scale generates seven modes which are scales that begin on the seven notes of the major scale and use that key signature to determine the relationship of whole steps and half steps. The first mode, ionian, is identical to the major scale. The second mode (in E-major), dorian, begins on the second note of the scale, F-sharp, and continues G-sharp, A, B, C-sharp, D-sharp, E, F-sharp. The third mode, phrygian begins on the third note of the scale, G-sharp, and continues A, B, C-sharp, D-sharp, E, F-sharp. Lydian begins on the fourth note, A, mixolydian on the fifth note, B, while aeolian is identical to the natural minor of E-major beginning on the sixth note, C-sharp, and locrian (which is rarely used) begins on the seventh note, D-sharp.

Most traditionally produced and tuned (I use this term loosely) Native American flutes do not have the full chromatic scale or equal spacing between pitches because of variations in production methods and woods. This makes using a European based fingering system somewhat problematic. However, in working with the Native American flute, I have found a series of Boehm-based fingerings that quite adequately cover the range of the basic and extended scales of many traditional flutes. Using the notational system of diatonic tuning as a basic road-map the individual sound footprints of tone and pitch step relationships are easily discernible and the variations in pitch relationships easily represented and understood.

In this book, all music for the Native American flute will be notated in four sharps which is the key signature for the E-major scale:

It is important

to be sure that

the fingertips

completely cover

each hole for good

tone production.

FIGURE 2. E-major scale.

FIGURE 3. Proper technique for blowing flute and placement of hands.

Now since all flutes do not work alike and beginning and ending pitches all differ somewhat, I have devised the following tablature system that uses the major portion of the E-major scale but starts on the lowest space of the five-lined staff (the F space). This system is easy to remember because the lowest tone along with its standard finger position are located just above the lowest line and no further down (this I equate to being on the surface of the Earth over which the sound of the flute will circulate like the seven sacred winds of native theosophy).

Remember that the note-like symbols indicate only what fingers to depress for either the five- or six-hole flutes to make a higher or lower sound as indicated by its position on the staff lines. In other words, this scale now becomes a *fingering tablature* and is not related to actual pitches in any way.

By starting from the lowest pitch of the woodlands Native American flute, the resulting scale tones are similar to the diatonic E-major/C-sharp minor scale [although this scale is nearly the same as the F-sharp dorian mode of E-major, the second degree (G-sharp) is missing in the modal scale of the six-hole flute]. It is important to note that not all Native American flutes work in the exact same tunings. If one is performing solos or duets on instruments of similar construction, treat the notation as a tablature or fingering guide realizing that pitches do not conform to the equal tempered scale (like the tuning one finds on a piano). Instead of reading music, you will only read symbols indicating what fingers to depress for a particular pitch within the arbitrary scale system of the flute.

However, the notational values and other mechanisms for standard notation serve the same function as they have always served: to indicate durations of time and overall melodic form. Thus, the fingering tablature serves a dual purpose that is easily understood by even those with minimal music training. Instead of reading music, you are only reading symbols that indicate what fingers to depress to achieve a pitch that may be higher or lower than previous pitches.

The most familiar scale is formed by simply covering all the tone holes to produce the lowest possible tone (i.e. the "fundamental") and then one by one lifting the fingers from bottom to top. The open holes provide a vent to the atmospheric air pressure which in effect shortens the "acoustic length" of the instrument. It is important to be sure that the fingertips completely cover each hole for good tone production (correct finger placement as well as arm position and embouchure are shown in Figures 3, 4, 5).

Because of variations in flute manufacture some tones will have an alternate finger position or the tone at one or more positions will not be playable.

FIGURE 4. Side view of proper fingering technique to create fundamental tone.

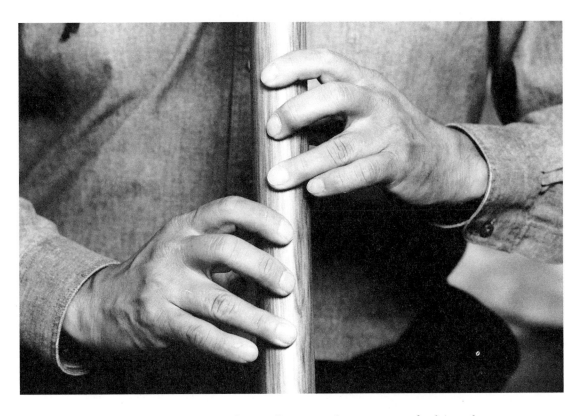

FIGURE 5. Top view of proper fingering technique to create fundamental tone.

By applying the first concept we are able to establish a primary scale with specific fingerings and some pitches that can be played in more than one way. The primary scale uses eight finger positions as shown in tablature for five and six-hole flutes.

A word of warning: Cross referencing and determining exact transpositional pitch relationships between the tablature and the actual sounded pitch will only result in extreme frustration because the same fingerings will result in different sounded pitches on different flutes. Because of variations in flute manufacture some tones will have an alternate finger position or the tone at one or more positions will not be playable.

FIGURE 6. Primary scale, 5-hole flute (based on Daniel Red Buffalo flute, circa 1930).

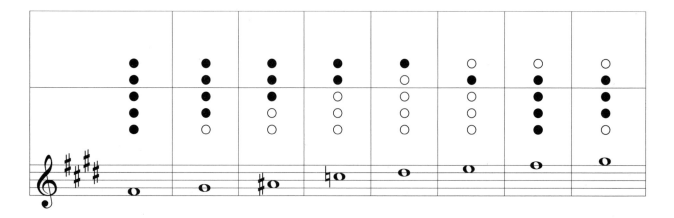

FIGURE 7. Primary scale, 6-hole flute

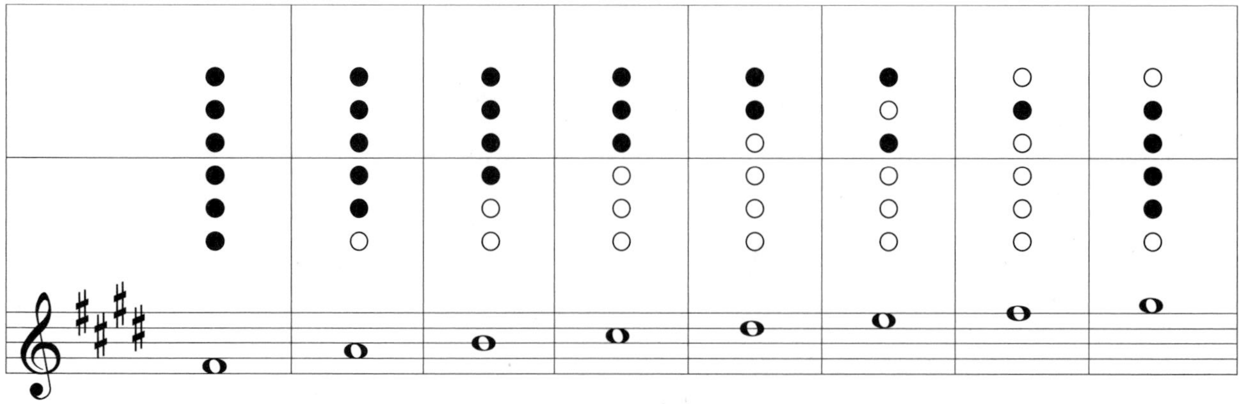

FIGURE 8. Fingering exercises for the 5-hole flute.

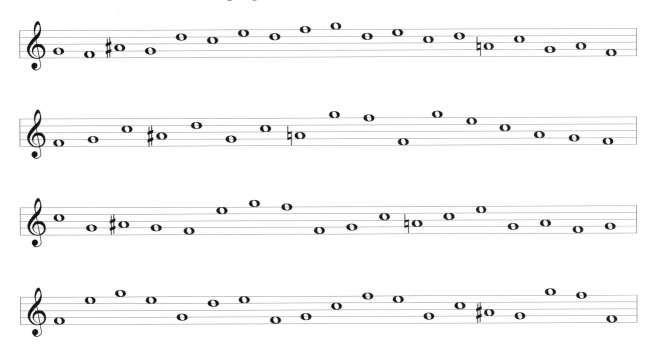

FIGURE 9. Fingering exercises for the 6-hole flute.

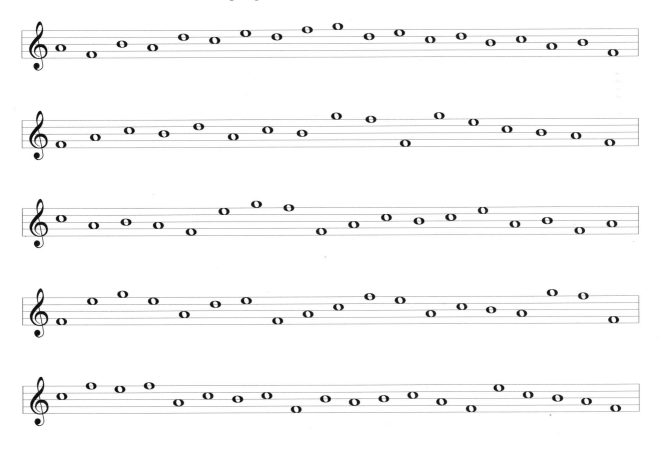

I recommend using the tablature notation only in cases where the flute will be used as a solo instrument.

If you have more than one flute, try playing these on the other flutes and note the differences in sounds. Once you've become comfortable with the primary scale, try the fingering exercises (Figures 8, 9) for the five-hole and six-hole flutes.

– 4 –

THE EXTENDED SCALE

NOW THAT YOU HAVE BECOME
COMFORTABLE WITH THE FUNDAMENTAL NOTES AND TONE PRODUC-
TION YOU MAY WISH TO FURTHER EXPLORE THE RESOURCES OF YOUR
instrument. As we said earlier the pitch of the flute depends on its "acoustic
length" which is analogous to the distance between the flue and the open
tone holes. You may have noticed that:

1. It is possible to lower a pitch by covering a hole below the open tone
   hole as is done for the high E and F-sharp, and
2. The pitch will gradually descend as you slowly move your finger to
   cover a tone hole (this is the wonderful asset of an instrument with
   open holes).

In both cases you are drawing the sound wave further down the instrument
before it reaches atmospheric pressure and reflects.

FIGURE 10. Extended scale, 5-hole flute.

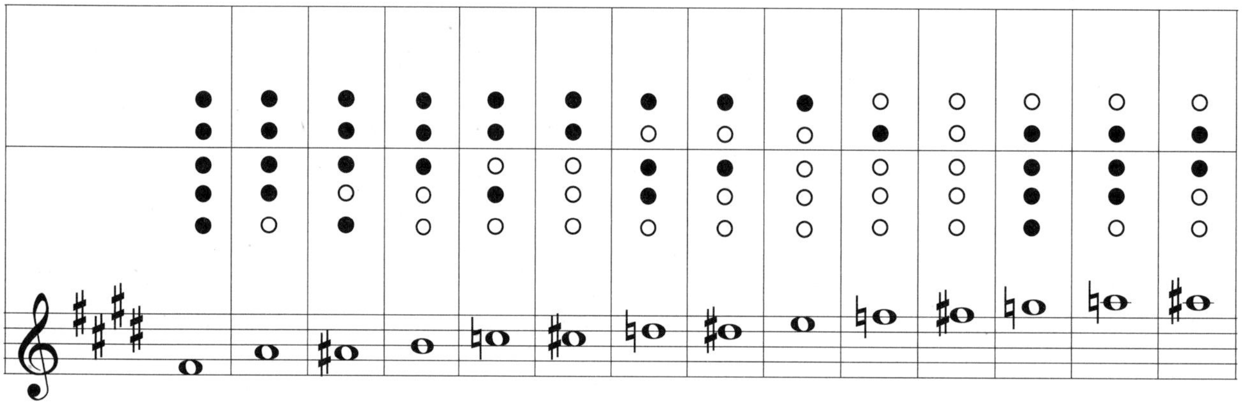

FIGURE 11. Extended scale, 6-hole flute.

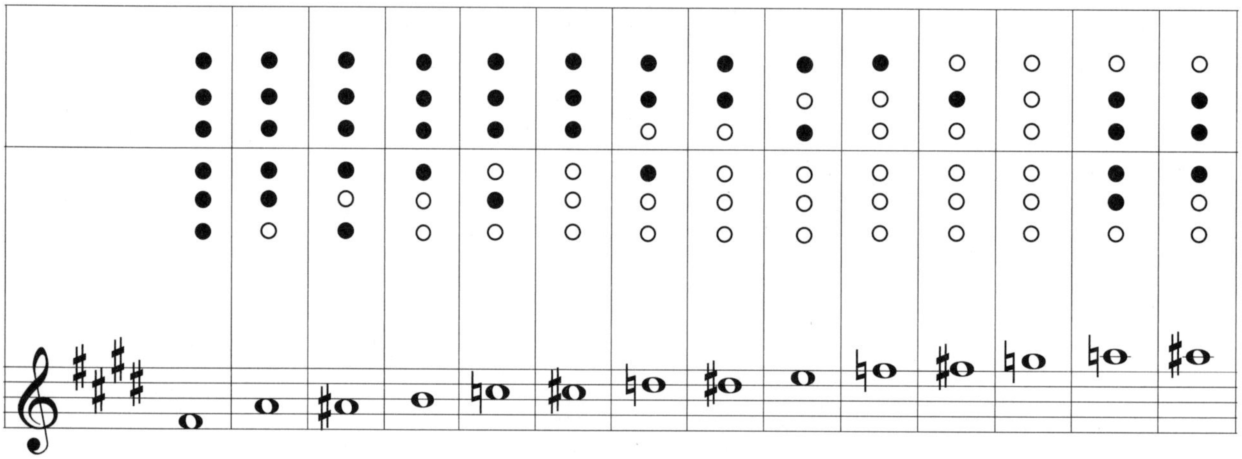

In working with the Native American flute, I have found a series of standard flute and recorder fingerings that includes all the possible standard pitches or *extended scale* of one or more flutes. The extended scale uses the eight basic finger positions and adds the notation for the half-steps between each of the primary tones. Only fully-closed finger positions are represented since any attempts at using half-closed finger positions are unreliable when near exact tuning is desired. In all cases where tablature is used, the sharp sign (♯) notation is also used for descending tones rather confusing the issue with the flat-sign (♭) for descending tones. Keep things as simple as possible!

Other finger positions, you may have already discovered, are substitutes for playing the standard pitches. These are called alternate positions. In many cases the alternate positions are just a little sharp or flat in pitch and are notated on a fingering guide with a plus (+) or a minus (-) sign as appropriate. The alternate fingering positions allow for variations in tone color, speed in fingering changes and are called for in some arrangements and are written below the tablature notation.

The alternate fingerings of D-sharp, F-sharp, and G are often used to provide easier fingering patterns for playing passing tones and rapid ornamental passages. This is most obvious when a rapid alteration between high G and G-sharp. You may also notice that the fingering for high F-sharp may be the same as that for low F-sharp. In order for the higher tone to sound, it is necessary to blow harder to increase the air speed so that the lower note is "over blown." When you do this you are causing the air column in the flute to flip into a higher mode of vibration (this is analogous to spinning a jump rope faster and causing two "humps" to form). Although this works well for the high F-sharp the technique of over-blowing tends to produce shrill, unstable notes for other pitches.

If you intend to play in ensembles which use the standard tempered tuning of European musical practice, you may find it necessary to pay close attention to how the pitch may change in accordance with the air speed; blowing harder will cause the pitch to rise. It is also important to remember that these fingerings may provide different results on instruments which have significantly different construction. If this is the case you can apply the principle of covering the holes below the vented hole to establish your own alternate tablature. Make sure that you write this new alternate (+, -) fingering tablature beside the standard ones shown.

This extremely reliable and theory-based method allows musician and instrumentalist alike to make sense of an arbitrary system of instrument making and sound production without the need for involved transposition, cross-fingering technique and other guess work commonly associated with hand-made wind instruments. The system of tablature notation also accommodates the actual pitch relationship of various instruments while using one fingering technique to indicate unplayable or alternate positions (as indicated in Figure 12).

Other systems of vocalizations, the *solfège* ("do-re-mi") system, the pentatonic scale (five tone system) and the middle-C based variations of tablature do not adequately serve the actual pitch relationships in this easy-to-see method. They tend to over-simplify and many times do not represent the actual pitch spacing of the Native American flute. Nor do the arbitrarily notated methods represent in a totally reliable manner a commonly understood usage for both the experienced and beginning musician.

Another word of warning: Again, the tendency, especially with professional performers, is to try to find a correlation between the actual pitches of their Native American flute(s) and the base F-line tablature. However, none exists except that of correctly notating the accidentals and alternate fingering positions for a particular instrument or musical arrangement.

I have been concerned with using a standard, time-tested flute fingering technique which will allow the performer to write for finger position rather than actual pitch. Figure 12 shows how finger position relates to actual pitch for one or more Native American flutes.

If you play in ensembles which use standard tuning, you may find it necessary to pay close attention to how the pitch may change in accordance with air speed.

OTHER KEYS AND TABLATURE RELATIONSHIPS

Because there are no standard lengths, bore diameter, placement of sound producing mechanisms or strict construction parameters, it is possible to find Native American flutes that have different fundamental notes. I am aware of six-hole flutes based on B/G-sharp minor, E/C-sharp minor, B-flat/G minor and C/A minor with flutes in B-flat/G minor and E/C-sharp minor the most popular. The B/G-sharp minor tuning has been attributed to the central and southern Plains tribes and the E/C-sharp minor tunings to the Great Lakes and woodlands tribes since their respective vocal music correlates to these tunings. Again, while the sounded pitches of the Native American flutes will have the sharps and flats of the major diatonic system, the root position (all finger holes closed) may begin higher or lower, thus indicating the instrument plays a modal scale.

FIGURE 12.

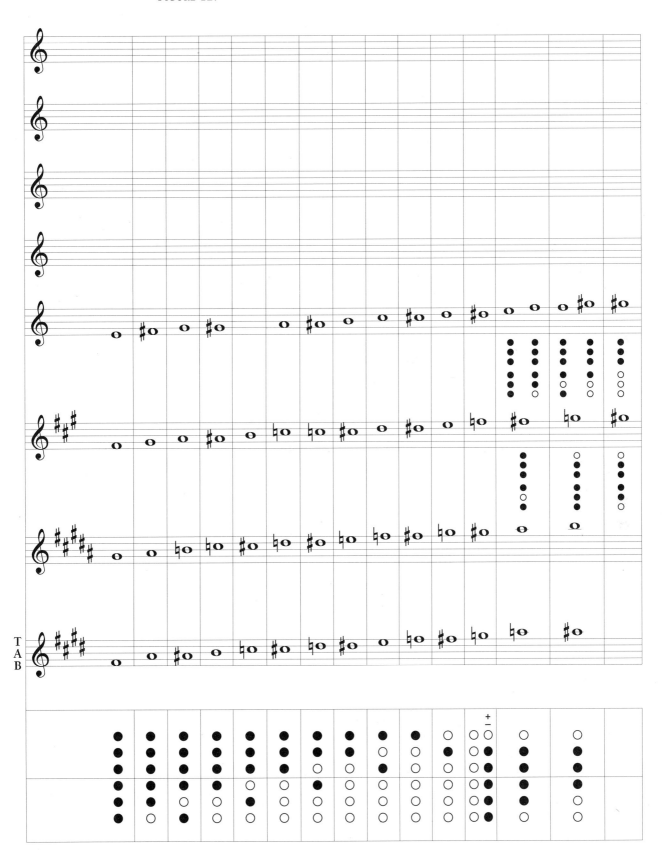

In an effort to simplify the transition from one flute to another (e.g., changing from a flute in F-sharp minor to G minor) I have maintained the same notation for all flutes. These instruments produce the same series of musical intervals as the F-sharp minor flute but the pitches are transposed so that the scale begins on the same fundamental tone. The lower tone is played with all finger holes closed and is written as F-sharp (F♯) but the actual sounded pitch will vary from one flute to another. The correlation of actual pitch to finger notation is easily and readily determined by cross-referencing the line for the key of your Native American flute and the column in which the tablature notation occurs. Each Native American flute uses the very same fingerings, from all-closed to middle three, and by using a digital tuner or well-tuned piano the actual pitch can be written in their exact notational positions over the tablature notation. The actual sounded pitch of the flute you are using can be organized into a gridwork pattern of correctly notated A440-based pitches (concert tuning in which the A below middle-C is tuned to 440 cycles per second) over the basic F-line tablature as shown in Figure 12.

Because the Native American flute is quite new to orchestral performance, we recommend when the flute is used with orchestral instruments that the flute part should be treated as a transposing instrument with the actual sounded pitches in the score and a separate part for the flutist using the tablature notation.

This knowledge is important when using actual chromatic notation as a guide for fingering notation for performance purposes. In any case, what pitch is sounded is not critical unless you intend to perform the melody with other musicians. Then, rather than playing what is written in actual pitch notation for the Native American flute part, the heretofore understood tablature notation is written along with the key signature for the actual pitch and what flute to use. This method will simplify notation (especially on the computer) and reduce the number of accidentals used.

WRITING AND ARRANGING IN TABLATURE FORM

From this arrangement of actual pitches the major scale or its minor key for each flute you own can be found using standard music theory. If you are composing a piece and need to know the actual pitch for the finger position

We are born with severe limitations and shortcomings as human beings. Finding ways to overcome them…is our personal task.

you are using there are two methods available:

Method One: Write everything in pencil in tablature notation and then use the grid to find the real pitches, make changes and write in permanent ink over the pencil marks which you can erase later.

Method Two: If you know the music and need to make an arrangement to play on your Native American flutes, then:

When the flute is used with orchestral instruments the flute part should be treated as a transposed instrument.

1. Find the extended scale of the five- or six-hole pitches that best fits the range of the song.

2. Find the lowest pitch in the original piece, count the spaces you will need to move that pitch to the F-line and move all the other notes in the song accordingly. (Most musicians count the starting notes as "1" then continue from there, but I have seen others start with the first space you will move to as "1".) For pitches far above the capabilities of your selected flute, write the highest pitches down an octave (eight steps lower) and continue with step 3.

3. Write the new arrangement in tablature notation and play it. Figure out what to do with sounds that are out of your range, unplayable sounds and how to correct an out of tune sound. If the piece is a solo rendition then find the best-sounding pitch relationship that will not detract from the piece.

By studying the melodies in Part II of this book you'll get a good idea of what to do in most cases. Here's where any amount of formal music training and ability comes in handy. The intent throughout this book and in the exercises is to correlate finger position to tablature notation without consideration of actual pitch notation. For those with minimal music training, writing original melodies based upon finger position rather than pitch is invaluable. For trained musicians, writing and composing in key and transposing the flute part to tablature notation while paying attention to the idiosyncrasies of the selected flutes allows for more control and application of pitch schemes outside of traditional forms. Control without having to work too hard is the key at all times.

Another word of warning: The Native American flute will only do what it's capable of doing and nothing more. Drilling half-stop holes beside the finger holes, filing on portions of the variable tube, using more than one flute and other innovations will either only make your flute unplayable or ruin your project all together. We are born with severe limitations and shortcomings as human beings. Finding ways to overcome them by using what's readily available is our personal task.

– 5 –

TRADITIONAL ORNAMENTS AND ENDINGS

As INDIVIDUAL ACTORS UPON THE STAGE OF VARIED LIFE, EACH OF US SEEKS A DEFINITIVE IDENTITY, BOTH FROM WITHIN (*HOW DO I SEE MYSELF?*) AND without (*How do others see me?*). The little variations we add to our personalities help us fix in the moment our complex and ever-changing individual identities. So too, the little variations in sound that we add to our playing increases our palette of sonic colorations and allows our individuality to be expressed through the voice of our flute.

In the following section these little variations in sound, through which we add ourselves to the music are outlined. These musical figures, ornaments and embellishments, and techniques of breath control, embouchure, and fingering are used throughout the world of music and are especially important to making a personally expressive presentation of Native American flute music.

Pitch Bend

By applying the technique of gradually raising or lowering the fingers it is possible to "bend" the pitch. This expressive gesture is often left to the discretion of the player since it has become an idiomatic characteristic of music performed on the Native American flute. Pitch bends are notated as follows:

FIGURE 13. GLISSANDO - a line connecting the starting and ending pitches and indicating that all available pitches between the two notes should be played in sequence as rapidly as possible.

FIGURE 14. DOIT - an ascending line following the note which indicates that the note is sounded and the finger is gradually lifted near the end of the note's duration.

FIGURE 15. FALL OFF - a descending line following the note which indicates that the note is sounded and the next finger is gradually lowered near the end of the note's duration.

FIGURE 16. SLIDE - an ascending or descending line ahead of the note which indicates that the performer should approach the note from above or below and slide into the written pitch.

Trills

Trills also often occur at the discretion of the player as a rapid alternation between two consecutive notes of the given melody. This technique is frequently employed when a musical phrase is repeated one or more times. The three trill symbols which we frequently use are:

FIGURE 17. TRILL - a wavy line which indicates a rapid alternation between the written note and the note a step above it.

FIGURE 18. MORDANT - a wavy line with a slash through it which indicates a rapid alternation between the note and the note a step below it. (Please note that we have adapted this baroque symbol and intend that it should mean nothing more than what is stated.)

FIGURE 19. TURN - a curved figure indicates a rapid alternation between the note and the notes a step above and below it.

Many other ornamental figures are developed by individual artists and become trademarks of their own personal style. If these ornaments are desired they should be written out in complete music notation the first time they are used and a musical symbol may be invented to indicate their repetition in other places in the music.

Flutter Tongue

The flutter tongue technique may be used to add interest to a melodic line by changing the nature of the tone. It is achieved by rolling an "r" ("rrrr") while blowing the flute. It can be very raucous when played loudly or in the high register or add mystery to a soft low passage. You may think of it as a spice which can be added at the end of a long sustained note just prior to changing to new note.

FIGURE 20. FLUTTER TONGUE - notated by placing three slashes through the stem of the note.

Double Tongue

This technique is a bit more challenging although it is related to flutter tonguing. In this case the effect is achieved by bouncing the tongue between the front and back of the palette in a rapid, regular fashion; as if you were saying "du-ku-du-ku-du-ku..." while playing the instrument. One advantage to double tonguing is that it can be accomplished at a softer level than flutter tonguing, especially in the lower register.

FIGURE 21. DOUBLE TONGUE - notated by placing two slashes through the stem of the note.

Many other ornamental figures are developed by individual artists and become trademarks of their own personal style.

— 6 —

STANDARD NOTATION AND VARIATIONS

TRADITIONALLY, MUSIC HAS BEEN TRANSMITTED ORALLY WITHIN THE NATIVE AMERICAN CULTURE PLACING MORE EMPHASIS ON THE RELATIONSHIP BETWEEN TEACHER and student, between elder and younger, upon communal needs and the skill of listening. The oral tradition would be the preferred way to teach the Native American flute but to communicate with as many as possible, I have chosen to use written words and written music.

Within European traditions music has been communicated with a written notation that allows for a broad dissemination of music and relies more on the skill of looking. What follows is a brief explanation of traditional European notation for those who have never encountered written music. After reading this section, if you are still not clear about European practice, I recommend you contact an experienced musician who can help explain some of the mysteries. If you are an experienced music reader you will want to jump ahead to the section on parlando style on page 41.

33

The different qualities of the music to be played—pitch, beat and rhythm, loudness and articulation—are communicated by a set of symbols written on a stave which is comprised of five lines. For treble instruments like the Native American flute, a G-clef or treble clef (Figure 22) indicates (by circling the second line from the bottom) where the G above middle C is located.

FIGURE 22. TREBLE CLEF

For lower pitched instruments (or voices), an F-clef or bass clef (Figure 23) indicates (by bracketing the second line from the top) where the F below middle C is located.

FIGURE 23. BASS CLEF

Instruments with broad ranges, like the piano or organ, use both clefs in tandem. Pitches normally used by treble instruments (or high voices) are named in Figure 24.

FIGURE 24. MIDDLE C

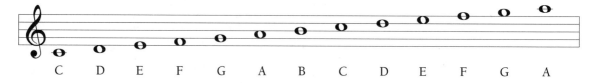

C   D   E   F   G   A   B   C   D   E   F   G   A

Certain symbols called *accidentals* indicate whether a note should be played a half step higher (*sharp*—notated as "♯") or a half step lower (*flat*—notated as "♭"). To cancel an accidental and return the note to its original pitch, a natural (notated as "♮") is used. Accidentals can be shown throughout the composition or are more commonly grouped at the beginning of the work in a *key signature*.

Key signatures indicate that those notes marked by a sharp or flat must be altered whenever the note occurs and in all octaves. Key signatures affect the note through the entire work unless a natural is placed before the note or a new key signature is shown. In standard European notation, sharps are always marked in the following order—F, C, G, D, A, E, B (Figure 25) and flats—B, E, A, D, G, C, F (Figure 26). Only on rare occasions are sharps and flats mixed in a key signature

FIGURE 25. Key signature showing order of sharps.

FIGURE 26. Key signature showing order of flats.

In standard rhythmic notation the beat is usually represented by a quarter note which may be divided by even or odd numbers. Possible divisions of the beat are demonstrated on the following chart along with the common name of each unit of subdivision:

FIGURE 27. THE BEAT

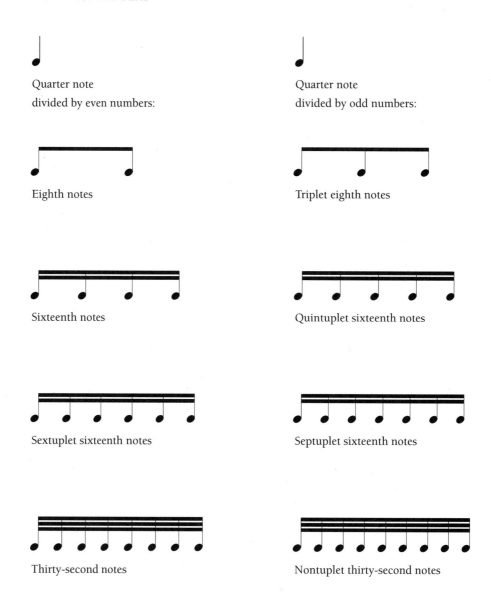

Quarter note
divided by even numbers:

Quarter note
divided by odd numbers:

Eighth notes

Triplet eighth notes

Sixteenth notes

Quintuplet sixteenth notes

Sextuplet sixteenth notes

Septuplet sixteenth notes

Thirty-second notes

Nontuplet thirty-second notes

Silence is notated in similar fashion based on the quarter rest.

FIGURE 28. RESTS

𝄽 = quarter rest

𝄾 = eighth rest

𝄿 = sixteenth rest

𝅀 = thirty-second rest

The basic beat and silence may also be multiplied in the following manner.

FIGURE 29. BEAT AND SILENCE (in 4/4 time)

♩ = quarter note (one beat)

♩ = half note (two beats)

𝐨 = whole note (four beats)

𝄽 = quarter rest (silence for one beat)

▬ = half rest (silence for two beats)

▬ = whole rest (silence for four beats)

Beats may be added together with the use of the *tie*. Ties are unnecessary when silences are added and therefore are never used with rests.

FIGURE 30. TIES

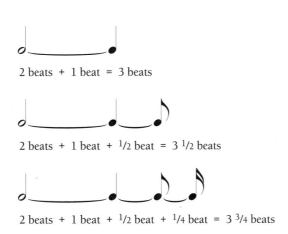

2 beats + 1 beat = 3 beats

2 beats + 1 beat + ¹/₂ beat = 3 ¹/₂ beats

2 beats + 1 beat + ¹/₂ beat + ¹/₄ beat = 3 ³/₄ beats

Ties are often used when beats are organized into groups which are called *measures* or *bars* which are separated by a vertical line called a *barline*. At the beginning of a piece a *time signature* tells you how many beats will occur in a measure and how the beat will be indicated. Most often beats are placed in groups of two (2/4 in which there are two beats per measure with the quarter note as the basic beat) or four (4/4 or four beats per measure with the quarter note as the basic beat). This grouping of number of beats and basic beat is called the *meter*.

FIGURE 31. THE METER

A useful shorthand replaces the tie with a dot placed after the note. This dot indicates that one half of the note value following is added to the note.

FIGURE 32.

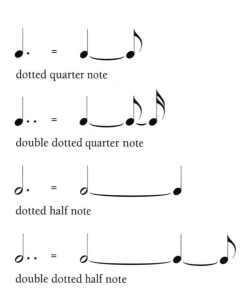

The following shows a correct use of the tie and an incorrect use of the dotted rhythm. In the second example the dotted rhythm cannot replace the first tie because it would result in more than four beats per bar.

FIGURE 33. Correct use of tie (top) and incorrect use of dotted rhythm (bottom).

Other meters are possible with the "simple" meters of 2/4, 3/4 and 4/4 most common and such meters as 5/4, 6/4 and 7/4 less common.

Figure 34. DIFFERENT METERS

Some meters are based on quarter note groupings known as "compound" meters. In these meters the dotted quarter note is the beat and is comprised of three eighth notes. The top note of the time signature will always be in multiples of three. Although the time signature of 6/8 seems to indicate that there are six beats in a measure and that the eighth note is the beat, in practice, musicians perform the music in two beats with each beat a dotted quarter note. A 9/8 time signature has three beats and a 12/8 time signature has four beats.

FIGURE 35. COMPOUND METERS

In addition to the basic rhythmic notation and pitch it is important to understand the following symbols for loudness and articulations (or how the note should be played).

FIGURE 36. DYNAMICS (Loudness)

mf   MEZZO FORTE (*met'-zoh for'-tay*) - average or medium level; meaning literally "half loud" in Italian

mp   MEZZO PIANO (*met'-zoh pee-an'-oh*) - softer than "*mf*"

p   PIANO (*pee-an'-oh*) - soft

pp   PIANISSIMO (*pee-a-nis'-i-moh*) - very soft

f   FORTE (*for'-tay*) - loud

ff   FORTISSIMO (*for-tis'-i-moh*) - very loud

sfz   SFORZANDO (*sfor-tsan'-do*) - a single note, loud

Figure 37. Articulations

> ACCENT - near the note head indicates that it should be played louder than normal.

. STACCATO - marking above or below the note head indicates that it should be played shorter than normal creating a brief silence before the following notes.

— TENUTO (*teh-new'-toh*) - marking above or below the note head indicates that it should be played with somewhat more emphasis than normal and sound for the full duration of the note.

⌢ FERMATA (*fur-mah'-tah*) - over a note indicates that it should last about twice as long as the notated duration. In ensemble playing, a cue is given by the conductor or leader signaling that the piece will continue.

⌇ ❜ CAESURA (*seh-zuhr'-ah*) - indicates a pause which breaks the flow of beats, thus requiring a cue to continue when playing in ensembles.

‖ DOUBLE BAR - indicates the end of the piece.

⦂‖ REPEAT SIGN - a pair of double bars which indicates that the music between the bars is to be played a second time.

PARLANDO STYLE AND NOTATION

Through rhythmic notation we attempt to recall the way we experience the rhythms of speech or movements of our body. It is important to realize that musicians seldom perform notated rhythms with computer-like precision. Standard rhythm notation is based on the concept of beats which are assumed to recur in a regular fashion. The flute however, grew from a tradition of poetic speech, and in speech there is no beating drum. Parlando notation is therefore, based on the parlando or "spoken" style and is presented here to encourage more exploration of this style.

Parlando notation reflects the freer rhythms of solo song by assuming a sense of a basic duration, written as a quarter note, which may be stretched by varying degrees (see Figure 38).

FIGURE 38. Durations may be stretched in varying degrees.

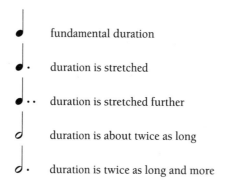

♩   fundamental duration

♩.   duration is stretched

♩..   duration is stretched further

♩   duration is about twice as long

♩.   duration is twice as long and more

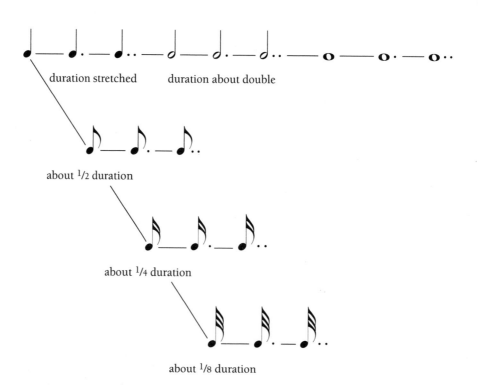

By interpreting these in a general sense we can better recall the feel of musical speech or solo song. The exercises in Figure 39 are written entirely in parlando style.

FIGURE 39. Exercise in parlando style.

The following passages mix parlando and traditional notation.

FIGURE 40. Parlando and traditional notation.

If you are comfortable with this concept it may help to achieve a similar freedom when confronted with "normal rhythms." For example, the notation on the left may be performed as either of the parlando notations shown on the right. This is a decision best left to the performer and is subject to change.

FIGURE 41. Original standard notation (left) with two parlando interpretations (right).

Interpretation #1

Original standard notation

Interpretation #2

Standard notation is convenient for works which involve more than one player (duets to full orchestra) and it is, of course, more familiar. Therefore, most works have been transcribed in standard notation. It should be understood, however, that when examples are given in standard rhythmic notation, it is intended that the performer will be searching for the *real* rhythm and take freedom in so doing. In collaborations parlando notation is reserved to imply a flexibility beyond the usual style. (For an example listen to "Lake That Speaks" from the Canyon Records recording, *Native Tapestry*).

MIXED METERS

In ensemble work, mixed meters have often been used to provide an undulating rhythmic background. These meters are groupings of simple and compound beats.

FIGURE 42. 7/8 is an example of a metric grouping of two quarter notes and one dotted quarter (2 + 2 + 3).

FIGURE 43. 8/8 is an example of a metric grouping of one quarter note and two dotted quarters (3 + 3 + 2).

FIGURE 44. 9/8 is an example of a metric grouping of one quarter note and two dotted quarters (3 + 2 + 2 + 2).

FIGURE 45. 10/8 is an example of a metric grouping of one quarter note and two dotted quarters (3 + 3 + 2 + 2).

Mixed meters may also be understood as transformations of familiar metric patterns. For example, the following 3/4 pattern may become a 7/8 or 8/8 pattern.

FIGURE 46. A meter of 3/4 transformed to 8/8 and 7/8.

Of course, it is also possible to transform a 4/4 pattern to a mixed meter of 9/8 or 10/8. This is shown in the following (Figure 42) two orchestral phrases from "Spirit Call" (the first movement of the *Two World Concerto for Native American flute and orchestra*); it is interesting that the 9/8 (3 + 2 + 2 + 2) feels like an acceleration of the earlier 10/8 (3 + 3 + 2 + 2) material.

FIGURE 47. Two orchestral phrases from "Spirit Call."

In the accompaniment rhythm in "Tapestry V" (for Native American flute, piano, cello, soprano saxophone and percussion), a 7/4 meter is transformed to a regular alternation of 8/8 and 10/8.

FIGURE 48. Rhythm in "Tapestry V."

In summary, mixed meters provide an alternative approach by which the elastic rhythms of the parlando style may be provided for larger ensembles when composing accompaniments for the Native American flute.

PART II

NATIVE AMERICAN FLUTE MELODIES

The following melodies are written in tablature form for Native American flute. For instruments other than the Amon Olorin Flutes Sonoran, Great Lakes or Little Dog tuning, either five- or six-hole, you may need to arrange the songs to fit the range of your personally selected instrument.

Have a good time and be One in peace. Haago'onee'.

— R. Carlos Nakai

"December Snow"
(from "Changes")

by R. Carlos Nakai

"12/13/82 Song"
(from "Changes")

by R. Carlos Nakai

"Wioste Olowan Inkpa taya"

(from "Changes")

traditional

"Wioste Olowan Tokiya"

(from "Changes")

traditional

"11/3/82 Song"

by R. Carlos Nakai

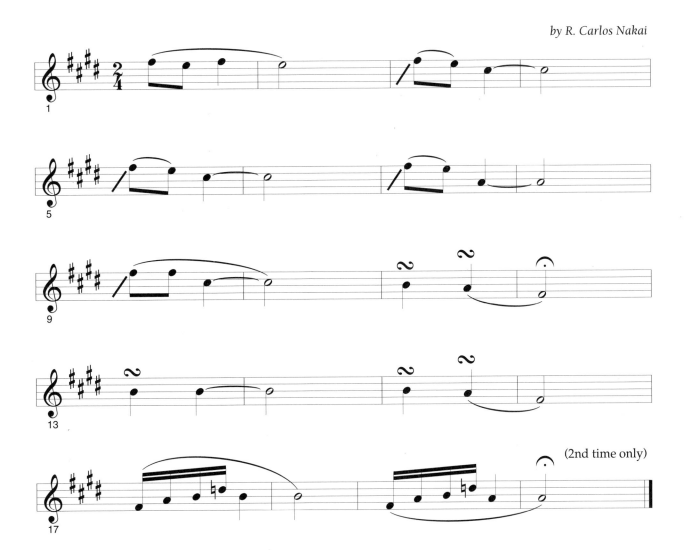

"Death Song - Lament"
(from "Changes")

by R. Carlos Nakai

"11/11/82 Song"
(from "Changes")

by R. Carlos Nakai

"Zuni Song"
(from "Changes")

traditional
arranged by R. Carlos Nakai

"12/20/82 Song"
(from "Changes")

by R. Carlos Nakai

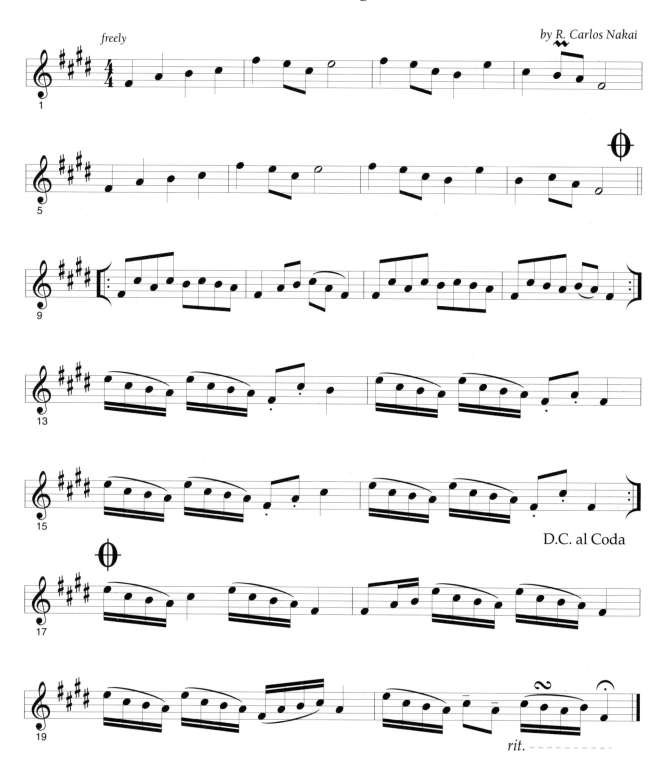

"12/13/82 Song"

(from "Changes")

by R. Carlos Nakai

"11/20/82 Song"
(from "Changes")

by R. Carlos Nakai

62

"Whippoorwill"
(from "Changes")

by R. Carlos Nakai

"Whirlwinds Dancing"
(from "Emergence")

by R. Carlos Nakai

"Coventry Carol"
(from "Winter Dreams")

c. 1500, traditional English
arranged by R. Carlos Nakai

D.C. al coda

"Rainy Nights in Taos"
(from "Journeys")

traditional
arranged by R. Carlos Nakai

"Omaha Song"
(from "Earth Spirit")

traditional
arranged by R. Carlos Nakai

67

"The Colors Fall"
Duet for Cedar Flute and Silver Flute (from "Spirit Horses")

by James DeMars

69

70

"Crow Wing"
Duet for Cedar Flute and E-flat Alto Saxophone
(from "Native Tapestry")

dedicated to
Joseph Marion D.

by James DeMars

73

75

THE

MUSIC

OF

R. CARLOS

NAKAI

BY

DAVID P.
MCALLESTER

— 1 —

THE BEGINNINGS OF A NEW GENRE

OST OF THE NEW GENRES OF NATIVE AMERICAN MUSIC IN THE 1980S WERE IN ROCK, GOSPEL, OR COUNTRY AND WESTERN FORMS, ACCORDING TO MCALLESTER and Mitchell in their 1983 article, "Navajo Music." There is another genre, which could be called "Indian message music," in which strikingly individual styles, usually with Euro-American instrumentation, convey the composer-performer's message to the Native American community and to the population at large. The music may make use of "traditional" Native American intervals, vocables, and drumbeats, and the texts extol values such as closeness to nature, spiritual awareness, generosity and friendship (McAllester 1981–82: 433–46).

Among these composer-performers, R. Carlos Nakai is among the very few who have worked with instrumental music as the primary medium. He was first trained as an instrumentalist in classical Euro-American music and he has worked consistently to find a place for the Native American flute in ensembles such as a jazz orchestra, a Western chamber orchestra, and other instrumentation from the world. He now has a mass audience, worldwide.

Other Native American orchestral composers include Louis W. Ballard, who like Nakai has also had a career teaching music in Indian schools (Ballard 1973). Ballard's principal vehicle is the Western orchestra. His works include *The Gods Will Hear,* a cantata for mixed chorus, vocal soloists, piano, and percussion; *Kachina Dances* for cello and chamber orchestra; *Why the Duck Has a Short Tail,* for narration and orchestra; and a woodwind quintet, *Ritmo Indio,* which won the MacDowell Award for American chamber music in 1969. Some of his works include orchestration for the "Sioux flute." His music is in the genre of "serious" or "art" music and is published as scores by at least two music publishers in New York City (Ballard 1973:84).

The rock, country and western, and other popular forms of new Native American music are also orchestral, of course, but the message is conveyed principally by extensive lyrics. However, a new genre of solo, traditional Native American flute music, inspired in part by Nakai's success, has begun to flourish in the last ten years. It may have had its beginnings in the 1970s when "Doc Tate" Nevaquaya made the first commercial recording consisting entirely of music of the Plains flute (Smythe 1989:68).

The wide interest caused by this recording was encouraged by Dr. Richard Payne, who had made Nevaquaya's flute and had given others to a number of younger players as well, including Nakai (Payne 1990). Payne, a non-Indian physician in Oklahoma City, is a notable collector and maker of all varieties of Native American flutes out of his long interest in music and Native American culture.

While some of the Oklahoma flutists have made original compositions in "traditional" style and have adapted hymn tunes to the flute, it is only recently that a few of them have begun to introduce bird calls and other "nature sounds" into their recordings and even create synthesizer accompaniments.

Nakai's innovativeness in this company of popular composer-performers can be seen in the degree to which he makes use of orchestral ensembles and other Euro-American accompaniments, and also in his sense of theater, organizing an entire album around a story or theme. He is unusual, also, in the articulateness with which he discusses his work in the album program notes from which much of this article has been drawn, and in interviews, lectures, workshops, and conferences for which he is in much demand.

. . . a new genre of solo, traditional Native American flute music, inspired in part by Nakai's success, has begun to flourish in the last ten years.

He is a poet, humorist, and environmentalist. He is also a philosopher with a universalist view of the arts and human relations.

R. Carlos Nakai is the oldest of the five children of Raymond Nakai, the former Navajo tribal chairman. "R.C." had studied education and music at Northern Arizona University in Flagstaff, his hometown, and had played classical Western trumpet there. He was also a jazz performer. But in 1973 his career took a different turn when he became acquainted with Native American flutes. Between then and the World Music Seminar in Woodstock, New York in 1982, he studied the background of these instruments, developed his own style of performance, and began teaching music in the schools on the Navajo reservation. He also produced his own tape, *Changes,* which was heard by Canyon Records and distributed by them in 1983. Since then he has released twenty four additional recordings, variously on LPs, cassettes and compact discs, and has captured the attention of an international audience. He has also been a major figure in a lively renaissance of Native American flute composition and performance.

Through the years Nakai has continued a steady progress of new projects and honors. He has toured Europe and Japan and earned a Master's degree in Native American Studies from the University of Arizona, the Arizona Governor's Arts Award in 1992 and an Honorary Doctorate from the University of Northern Arizona in 1994 and recognition from the First Americans in the Arts for his body of work in 1995. In 1994 his *Ancestral Voices* (with William Eaton) was a Grammy Awards finalist for "Best Traditional Folk Music." He has performed with a number of symphony orchestras and has recorded with an ever widening circle of musical collaborators. His goal of finding a role for the Native American flute in multicultural and multimusical settings finds further realization every year.

THE RECORDINGS OF R. CARLOS NAKAI

Nakai's recordings are listed in chronological order on the following page as a kind of reader's (or listener's) guide. I will discuss them *seriatim,* quoting from Nakai's own words in liner notes and interviews. Though space will not permit anything like the detailed examination they deserve, I will venture some thoughts on the place of R. Carlos Nakai among other contemporary Native Americans who are composers and performers.

Nakai is a poet, humorist, and environmentalist. He is also a philosopher with a universalist view of the arts and human relations.

R. Carlos Nakai Discography

1983	*Changes*	Canyon Records	(CR-615)
1985	*Cycles*	Canyon Records	(CR-614)
1986	*Journeys*	Canyon Records	(CR-613)
	Jackalope	Canyon Records	(CR-7001)
1987	*Earth Spirit*	Canyon Records	(CR-612)
1988	*Weavings*	Canyon Records	(CR-7002)
	Carry the Gift	Canyon Records	(CR-7006)
	Sundance Season	Celestial Harmonies	(13024)
1989	*Canyon Trilogy*	Canyon Records	(CR-610)
1990	*Natives*	Silver Wave Records	(SC-601)
	Winter Dreams	Canyon Records	(CR-7007)
	Desert Dance	Celestial Harmonies	(13033)
	Atlantic Crossing	Alter Pfarrhof Produktion	
1991	*Spirit Horses*	Canyon Records	(CR-615)
1992	*Migration*	Silver Wave Records	(SC-704)
	Ancestral Voices	Canyon Records	(CR-7010)
	Emergence	Canyon Records	(CR-609)
1993	*How the West Was Lost*	Silver Wave Records	(SC-801)
	Boat People	Canyon Records	(CR-7003)
1994	*Native Tapestry*	Canyon Records	(CR-7015)
	Dances with Rabbits	Canyon Records	(CR-7005)
	Island of Bows	Canyon Records	(CR-7018)
	Honorable Sky	Silver Wave Records	(SD-807)
1995	*How the West Was Lost II*	Silver Wave Records	(SD-901)
	Feather, Stone & Light	Canyon Records	(CR-7011)

DISCUSSION OF THE RECORDINGS

Changes, 1983.

This first volume establishes a tradition developed throughout the oeuvre: inspiration from a highly eclectic array of sources, identified for the listener by Nakai in brief, evocative, poetic notes. The title, *Changes,* suggests Nakai's variations on the melodic sources and, perhaps, his transformations from the visual to the musical and, in the notes, to the literary.

Changes is labeled by the record company as "An Experience in Tranquility." The first piece is "Zuni Song," an "embellishment of a traditional Zuni melody . . . [sung] at sunrise to greet the beginning of a new day." The rhythmically free way in which Nakai plays this melody sets the pattern for the other cuts on the recording. The smooth, mellow flow of sound provides, as the notes say, "a soothing, restful atmosphere. The artist paints by it. The psychiatrist employs it to provide an aura of pleasantness and peacefulness. It can help solve the cares of the day during a time of meditation."

This historic melody is one of the best known Indian songs in the country. Carlos Troyer published it as sheet music (Troyer 1913) and it has been reprinted widely in various versions in music books for school children and the Scouting movement ever since (Boardman and Landis 1966:140).

Nakai's music often celebrates special places. The next piece on the album, "Whippoorwill," is based on a whippoorwill song heard at Woodstock. Its premiere was played by Nakai with a jazz orchestra there. Other pieces in *Changes* were inspired by the dramatic scenery in Monument Valley, Lukachukai, and the San Francisco Peaks in Arizona. "Impressions of Atitlan" was composed after Nakai watched a gathering storm at evening in Guatemala. Two cuts are based on Lakota melodies found in a Bulletin of the Bureau of American Ethnology (Densmore 1918) and one is based on a Blood round dance. Two are based on European melodies, a medieval dance and a sea chantey.

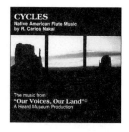

Cycles, 1985.

This was the soundtrack for the Heard Museum multimedia show "Our Voices, Our Land." I had the good fortune to see and hear this program in November 1988. Slides showed scene after scene of Southwestern landscapes and Pueblo ruins in luminous color, while a synthesizer accompaniment provided a pedal point so deep that one could imagine the rocks, the wide spaces, and the ancient buildings speaking in primordial tones. Narrow-ranged flute melodies incorporating Native American intonations and the frequent use of minor thirds all provided Indian "markers."

Nakai's titles and explanations of the pieces given in the notes focus on life forces:

> *"Cries" - the living planet and solar radiation provides a background fabric over which the cries of the shaman are voiced.*
>
> *"Elements" - the power of the wind and water are eternal. Prayerful utterances to the deities of life, of sustenance, of growth demonstrate the need for water and the action of the wind.*
>
> *"Origins" - my clan, Naashteezhi dine-e Taachiinii, allows me to be one of the People.*
>
> *"Shelter" - mothering is life, security and shelter. Heart and enclosure energy sounds are our first experience of this reality.*
>
> *"Ritual" - the beating of the heart and the buzzing energy of the mind are embellished with our sounds in prayer to the Power.*
>
> *"Creativity" - basic rhythmic structure and form allows the spirit force to create freely.*
>
> *"Whippoorwill" is a joint effort by Langhi and Nakai and originated at the Creative Music Studio in Woodstock, New York.*
>
> *"Future/Past" - where have we been, where are we going, and what are we doing?*
>
> *"Cycles" - filling the void are cycles of life energy. Our sensitivity to these patterns is harmony.*

Concerning the Heard Museum exhibit and Nakai, himself, the record notes have this to say: "Our Voices, Our Land" expresses the thoughts and feelings of Native Americans of the Southwest about their cultural traditions, lives and future. This presentation is part of the exhibit, "Native Peoples of the Southwest: The Permanent Collection of the Heard Museum," which highlights 15,000 years of history and cultural heritage of the Southwest....

Nakai's message in these statements is similar to those in the narration of A. Paul Ortega in his music, but with a different vocabulary, and to the texts of the music of Arliene Nofchissey Williams, Buddy Redbow, and others in a genre I have called "Indian message music" (1981–82). However, Nakai's work is unusual among these in several ways. For one thing, the text is written rather than narrated or sung. Another difference is the "New Age" musical vocabulary. In this recording, Nakai integrates musical forms and performance techniques of the Native American flute with his own original interpretations:

> The music of Cycles is based on sound experiences and sub-sonic vibrations that I have felt while on the vast expanses of the Northern Plains and Southwest. These sound experiences are perceived when in harmony with the cycles of life. Natural sounds are not tuned to a common tonality. Using Yamaha DX7 and Sequential Circuits Six-Track synthesizers, I express my experiences in the key of G-major and its relative minor modes to realize harmonic structures that incorporate melodies of the Native American flute.

Nakai goes on to say that the eight compositions that make up *Cycles* describe "Earth/Mind consciousness." The reader is reminded that five selections from this album provided the music for the ballet *Night Chant*, created by the Martha Graham Dance Company. A review in *New York Times* notes that Isamu Noguchi designed the sets and describes the climactic episode in the dance:

> Suddenly but serenely, the petroglyphs, or abstract stone representations of birds, found in the Southwest seemed mysteriously to cross a dark sky. They were in fact three seemingly headless women carried upside down on their partners' shoulders with legs bent upward, they were barely recognizable as human. A sculptor of the human body, Miss Graham had molded these dancers into mythic and anthropomorphic forms (Kisselgoff 1988).

By his second album, Nakai has brought the Native American flute into artistic conjunction with some of the most creative minds in the United States cultural mainstream. When I asked Nakai if he felt any contradiction between contemporary electronic technology and primordial earth vibrations, he said, "What could be more basic than metal and electricity?"

...sound experiences and subsonic vibrations that I have felt while on the vast expanses of the Northern Plains and Southwest.

Journeys, 1986.

This album is introduced by a poem:

> *At birth we embark on a good journey*
> *seeking a destination of happiness.*
> *The journeys on our life-road*
> *facilitate development of our*
> *emotional, mental, physical and*
> *spiritual states-of-being into a*
> *way of true power and wisdom.*
> *The Heart-center power, expressed as*
> *happiness and love will guide us*
> *upward on a path away from frustration,*
> *bitter toil and travail.*
>
> *These journeys are directed inward,*
> *not outwardly in material mementos of*
> *ego and possession.*
> *The lesson is relearning that which*
> *has been suppressed and forgotten,*
> *in ourselves, since our earliest*
> *childhood.*

One theme in this album is education in Native American music for children. It seems to be an expression of the many residencies, workshops, and teaching jobs in which Nakai has presented his ideas and music in the schools of Arizona and elsewhere. The first piece, "Life is for Living," is a game in which the title is spelled out melodically. One can imagine children of any age, including John Cage, enjoying this puzzle. The third piece, "Children's Song," rings variations on a song for a "Futures for Children" program. All of these pieces share a 1-3b-5, and a 1-3b-4-5 movement.

"Children's Dance," with its waltz rhythm and simple melodic structure, makes us notice how most of the other songs on the tape are comparatively free rhythmically and melodically and are probably improvised. This dance-like piece, "a song to play by," reminds one of the folk-art music of Carlos Chavez. "Rainy Nights in Taos" is the only melody on this tape stated to be an adaptation of a Native American song: "a traditional Southern Plains melody."

"The Rez Bunnies" is inspired by "my friends who live in the Chuska Mountains" (on the Navajo Reservation near Lukachukai). A deep bass synthesizer drone on the tonic note continues throughout the piece. A piano-like arpeggiation comes in near the beginning and also continues for the rest of the piece. By electronic means, the flute plays an improvisatory duet with itself.

The second side is entitled "Seven Improvisations": these improvisations, performed November 23, 1985, "incorporate the sounds of each of my working flutes as well as voice and synthesizers." They are all arhythmic, meditative, "soothing." No. 4 has a wind sound, probably from the synthesizer. No. 5 has wind, and a voice singing vocables. The last cut includes wind, waves, and sea-birds.

Jackalope, 1986.

Jackalope is a major collaborative work and a *jeu desprit*. Nakai, playing flutes, trumpet, and percussion, joins forces with Larry Yañez, a fellow worker with the Arizona Commission on the Arts, a musician, sculptor, and member of Movimiento Artisticos del Rio Salado. To Yañez's synthesizer and percussion is added the guitar, percussion, and E-flat washboard of Steve Cheseborough.

The album is not just a collection of pieces but a unified work, musically and ideationally. First we are introduced to the Jackalope theme in "Theme Song." It begins with a wind sound, synthesizer bird cries, and then a rapid, beeping 1-8-5-8, 1-8-5-8, and the theme: the chords on 3-2, 3-2, 1-2-3 in the pentatonic scale that characterizes the whole album.

This music, styled in the publicity as "New Age Jazz," is strictly rhythmic. The notes say that it:

> *...combines Native American melodies and ancient rhythms*
> *with hi-tech sounds. Flutes, brass and shell trumpets, whistles,*
> *game calls, shakers, and handmade drums blend with guitar and*
> *synthesizer to create SynthacousticpunkarachiNavajazz.*

One could say that Nakai's impulse to bring together things from diverse sources finds its full expression with these collaborators and their joint creation.

The Jackalope theme is elaborated in "G-minor Improvisation." The notes also tell us that Jackalope's music is improvisatory. We then come to "Roadkill," "the transition of a jackalope to the nether world." The theme returns with "wa-wa" synthesizer chords, electronically enriched melodic lines, and a jazz drum beat. One becomes aware of a strong pentatonic effect and then a remarkable evocation of the *sho,* the Japanese mouth organ. Overall the effect is funereal as befits the death of Jackalope.

"Festival of the Cow" is "...dedicated to large grazing animals who mill about in large groups as they eat (i.e.cows, college students at daytime concerts, cocktail partygoers)." The plangent chords of the Jackalope theme run all through the piece and it ends as it began with a jazzy tock-tock rhythm, slowly fading.

Side B introduces us to the alter egos of Nakai (Dog Soldier) and Yañez (Lord Fumamota). The first piece, "Macho Piccho," is about the "fabled home of Lord Fumamota." Since the notes are riddled with puns it seems justifiable to assume that Macchu Pichu has been altered to express Chicano masculinity and that Lord Fumamota smokes. The Jackalope themes are present with a jazz guitar behind them. "Lord Fumamota" is identified as a "Chicano samurai . . . immortalized in Yañez' multimedia work, 'Las Adventuras de Fumamota.'" We hear strings with a wide vibrato like the Japanese *koto* that fortify the impression of Japan produced earlier by pentatonicism and the *sho* sound. The fact that Nakai's flute has much the same timbre as the Japanese end-blown flute, the *shakuhachi*, adds to the impression.

"Coyote Mint" is "the theme of 'Dog Soldier' in an urban setting," and we are back on the chords on 3-2-3-2, 3-2-3-1. "Dog Leather" has the note "the eventual occurrence of roadkill," and seems to identify Dog Soldier (Nakai) with Jackalope. This can also be seen in the notes' definition of what a jackalope is: ". . . *lepus antilocapra erectus* is an elusive creature sometimes seen along the highways of the American Southwest. Some zoologists classify it as a cross between a jackrabbit and an antelope. . . . The music on this album was inspired by that extraordinary creature." The *erectus* puts our creature up on two legs.

...Nakai's impulse to bring together things from diverse sources finds its full expression with these collaborators and their joint creation.

Earth Spirit, 1987.

This recording is confined to wind instruments, at least two different flutes and an eagle-bone whistle. All of the music is in the characteristic arhythmic style with long-held notes expressively modulated and often ended with an overblown grace-note. An introductory paragraph explicates the title:

> *On the surface of "Snake Island" the time-worn beauty of Earth Mother is furrowed, like the cerebral cortex, by deep mysterious canyons whose awe-inspiring chasms inexorably provoke the musings of voyagers and storytellers. Seeps of mineral-laden water etch immense abstract patterns upon the vertical weather-worn canvas of Navajo sandstone, becoming representations of Yei and other*

*mythic beings. For countless centuries diné (people) have marveled
at the petroglyphs and pictographs chronicling events among the
ancient people.*

Again, Nakai's strong concern with place is evident in the pieces
inspired by visits to St. Louis, Beardstown in Illinois, Canyon de Chelly,
and Monument Valley. "Nemi," taken from Frazer's *The Golden Bough*,
refers to a grove of stone formations in Monument Valley (Nakai 1990).
Three other classical references in the titles are "In Medias Res," "Coyote
Animus," and "Aura Aurealis."

Nakai's pleasure in word-play surfaces and flourishes in the Jackalope
recordings. The many inspirations from nature can be seen in the references
to canyons, coyotes, catfish, stars, Earth and Sky, among others, in song
titles and in the notes. Each side ends with a piece on the eagle-bone whistle,
with high piccolo-like notes. "Song of the Evening Star" is "traditional
Kiowa, arranged from ethnomusicological notes by Frances Densmore," and
two other pieces draw directly from other Native American music: "Omaha
Song," from a transcription by Charles Wakefield Cadman, and "Athabascan
Song" from a record album published by the Wheelwright Museum in Santa
Fe and Peabody Museum of Harvard University, *Navajo Creation Chants*
(Wheelwright and McAllester 1952). The song is "When They Saw Each
Other," about the first meeting of Changing Woman and the Sun. Here
Nakai's arrangement keeps close to the original so that we hear more of
a "tune" and consistent rhythmic patterns than in most of his music.

Again we see Nakai's wide range of choices in time and space for
sources of inspiration in his music. He has a world perspective and he
makes it clear that Native American instruments and musics, and other
musics anywhere, can inform each other to the benefit of both.

Weavings, 1988.

The seriocomic legend, begun in *Jackalope,* is continued in this second
album with an antic journey, reminiscent of the quests in Native American
mythology. In "Dog Soldier," Nakai's alter ego "…leaves the Rez (reservation)
and journeys into the outer world attired in his best traditional dress.
However, this persona creates antagonistic defensive responses and he
adopts the persona of the *Wise One-Coyote* in order to move safely within
the outer world." The identity of Coyote-Dog Soldier-Jackalope-Nakai
is further established by these notes and we see that the part rabbit, part
antelope stands for all hyphenated Americans, as well.

The music is very different from that of the first Jackalope album: it is rhythmic throughout; invention and liveliness are everywhere. Nakai's trumpet has its turn, with an impressive soaring sound. Electronic bird simulations are heard. The Jackalope theme seems to be absent at first but it is subtly touched upon, again and again, and returns in full force in "Tezcatlipolka," when we hear it stated by Nakai's flute, mellow, quavering, soothing. We hear rattles, voices saying something inaudible. A "bullfrog" pedalpoint, 7-6-8, 7-6-8, runs through the piece which, incidentally, is not a polka.

The story is that Dog Soldier meets Lord Fumamota, "...they exchange stories. Dog Soldier's story is of his people's traditional homeland, Canada." We hear "God Save the Queen," also the title of the second piece, woven into the energetic jazz. Nakai says in the Artists' Statements: "The living tradition of the Diné ("people" or Navajo) is the weavings of gossamer threads in story, song, and visual arts to form a personalized oral tradition that reflects one's passage through AZTLAN." Then the serious side of this work emerges, Nakai's first overt protest statement in these recordings:

> For me, Jackalope is the restatement, in contemporary terms, of an awareness of the humanity of my culture and my own perspectives regarding the romantic stereotyping and social isolation plaguing Diné today. I always say, "We're still here after 200 years of suppression. Diné biláá asdlaii" [People/here/tarrying].

The rest of the story on side A is that the two heroes visit the Nauga tribe on their journey (their product, the hide of the nauga "is essential to many applications of twentieth century culture and art"). They get into an obsidian knife fight in Tenochtitlan and meet two other alter egos, Haiteca-Manteca (Richard Carbajal) and Waspteca (Darrell Flint). They are ordered to leave Tenochtitlan (the ancient name of Mexico City) and they do so to the farewell cries of Bullfrog and other tropical fauna. They begin "the search for the great landbridge between Snake Island and the outer world."

Side B takes the travelers north to a land of ice and snow. The piece, "Ihuela Cafroni" (a Chicano street epithet), is reminiscent of the slow parts of Copland's *Appalachian Spring*, with long sustained chords—a kind of arctic slow-motion. In "Meet Me at the Bering Strait," we hear elephantine trumpeting and chaotic noises with cymbals. "This is one of the greatest Woolly mammoth hunting grounds in the western hemisphere. Bring your camera!" Word arrives that tourists have come to the "land of Maya" (surely

He has a world perspective and he makes it clear that Native American instruments and musics, and other musics anywhere, can inform each other to the benefit of both.

there is reference here to illusion as well as the Mayans) and then in the last piece, "Then There Was Wood," the travelers hear that the tourists have brought diseases and horses and have taken over the neighborhood. A gentle vocal chorus, birds and other jungle sounds, and panpipes join in a lament for the fall of the Mexican Empire. The Jackalope motive, 1-7-6, 1-7-6, reappears, and a big Fu Manchu gong ends the album.

It is entertaining, but also poignant to have the album-legend end at the landbridge where the "Native American" saga began. The universalist perspective, a signature of Nakai's work, is significantly expanded here, in time and space.

Carry the Gift, 1988.

The title of this album refers, in part, to the dedication of Nakai and his collaborator William Eaton to teaching. The liner notes state:

> *Nakai and Eaton are educators as well as musicians and serve in
> the Artists-in-Education program for the Arizona Commission on
> the Arts. Their role as educators influences their work as musicians
> and composers. Carry the Gift reflects the philosophies of its two
> artists who view their artistic vision and cultural heritages as gifts
> to share with their listeners, gifts that teach as well as inspire....*

Collaborative work comes naturally to Nakai. In addition to the ensemble work in the Jackalope recordings discussed above, the reader will remember that "Whippoorwill" was first performed in a jazz ensemble at the World Music Seminar in 1982. Nakai's premiere of *Spirit Horses,* with chamber orchestra, also mentioned above, took place in 1986. In this new collaboration the sensitive string accompaniments by Eaton are something new again in Nakai's career. Also new (to the world) are some of Eaton's instruments. He is a luthier as well as a performer, and his principal instrument on this recording is the harp guitar of his own manufacture. He also plays the traditional guitar and the Brazilian *berimbau.* In addition, we hear sounds of wind, bird calls, water, echo chamber, vocal chanting, whistles, and synthesizer (which may have produced some of the above, as well as a deep drone underpinning).

Instead of notes explaining sources of the individual pieces, this album fulfills the literary promise of the poetry in some of the previous albums: there is now an explicatory poem with each cut. They are credited to William Eaton, Michael Barry, and R. Carlos Nakai.

Taken together with the music and other sound effects, this series of fifteen poems could be seen, like the Jackalope recordings, as music-theater. In an interesting way, the texts develop the themes of time passing during which birth, growing up, enculturation, hunting, warfare, and death take place. Several poems refer to the extinction of the deer, the drying up of the water, and the uncertainty of the future. The poem (by Michael Barry) with "Ten Winters" encapsulates the literary material as a whole:

> One's life is made in ten winters
> 1. From frozen seed beneath earth
> 2. this one sprouts
> 3. gathers light
> 4. makes, walks, dances, does
> 5. makes life
> 6. watches life grow
> 7. watches life grow
> 8. watches life go
> 9. breathes out final words
> 10. into frozen snow seed for tomorrow.

In the last piece, "Carry the Gift," Eaton's gentle arpeggios and Nakai's solemn flute fade out in echoing space while an occasional bird calls and, finally, we hear nothing but the wind. The accompanying poem, which has to be considered part of the art form, tells us that "The young one/sees the path/follows without hesitation/brings the light of ten winters/to those who come after."

The universalist

perspective,

a signature of

Nakai's work,

is significantly

expanded here, in

time and space.

Sundance Season, 1988.

This is the first of Nakai's albums to be published under a new label. It is a measure of Nakai's success with the general public that other companies, not specializing in Native American music, now seek to produce his work. Celestial Harmonies, in Tucson, Arizona, does focus on spiritual and New Age music. In their introduction to this album they say "...it [is] our wish to bring forth the 'Native People's' music as it is today to the other 'peoples' of the world, to renew the reverence and rejoice the Spirit. "

Sundance Season was recorded in July 1987 at the Lindisfarne Chapel, Lindisfarne Mountain Retreat, Crestone, Colorado. The album got its title almost casually: "...during a break in the recording sessions, the engineer, Stephen Hill, Carlos and myself (Ruby McFarland, project coordinator) saw a poster in a local restaurant advertising the annual Ute Sun Dance ceremony. We…knew we had a concept and a title for the project."

The album is a continuation of Nakai's popular "mood" pieces, with the soothing flute "smoothing the wrinkles of my mind," as one listener wrote. Again, many of the pieces draw their inspiration from the potent scenery of the Colorado Rockies. Nakai's evocative notes supplement the music: "the land of rugged eternal beauty," "the flight of the Golden Eagle over mountain ranges," "the awesome timelessness and spectacular juniper scented beauty of this land where my ancestors once roamed," "the celebratory blaze of sunset over the mountain bedecked horizon," "contemplating the gentle sounds of a mid-summer shower in the mountains.

The notes and publicity with the recording are unusually extensive: ten pages folded up into the box. The five back pages contain information about the Sun Dance: "The religious focus of this redemptive ritual includes conscious acknowledgement of the inclusiveness of all life on the Earth Mother upon whom the harmonious survival and well-being of all living things depends." There is a short bibliography of popular and scholarly works on the Sun Dance, and a discussion of the Native American flute with a diagram showing the structure of a Plains flute and two types of scales. Nakai also discusses the kind of notation he uses:

> *In practice I use a general notation related to the fingering pattern common to the instrument to sketch melodic passages. Key signatures or letter references assist me in describing the proper key in which to improvise when working with an ensemble; or which flute is best suited to a particular performance piece. This basic notation keeps the format of each piece intact and allows for improvisations while incorporating effects, dynamic figures and other techniques common to Native American flute performances. No formal method of practice is established by flutists within the indigenous culture, except that which allows the reinterpretation to be free-sounding and as melodically soothing as practicable. The melodies for Native American flute are loosely structured in the format of traditional vocal music and many melodies are derived from vocalization of traditional songs; hence the insistence that the flute be tuned by the maker as close to the natural human voice as possible.*

Side B of the recording ends with "Ritual I" and "Ritual II," which include Tibetan bells, voice singing vocables, rattle, another voice and, at the end, a little drumming. The rituals acknowledge "our inclusive affinity with all of Gaia." A coda at the end, on the eagle-bone whistle, is a prayer in which "the petitioner asks for eternal dialogue with the Great Mystery."

…the awesome timelessness and spectacular juniper scented beauty of this land where my ancestors once roamed…

Canyon Trilogy, 1989.

Here Nakai adds to the repertory of flute meditations that are his most popular works. For the first time the literary side of the production is missing, except for a general statement:

> The music in this trilogy reflects my impressions upon viewing ancient Anasazi and Sinagua sites in the Southwest. These cliff-dwellings with their pictographic histories continue to stir my imagination about this new mythical world.
>
> My inward musings and dreamscapes are reflected in this recording of solo flute melodies for you also to dream by. On this recording I have used the Roland SDE 3000 Digital Delay unit to simulate the ambiance of the canyons and valleys of these now abandoned villages.

Natives, 1990.

The album is another collaborative production, and again it is by a record company other than Canyon Records. Peter Kater, also the producer, accompanies Nakai on the piano. The notes indicate that sales from this recording benefited the United Nations Environment Program, and that Peter Kater assisted the same program in Earth Year 1990, on a sixty-city tour presented by the Arts and Entertainment Council of the United Nations. The notes are minimal: "This album is an improvisational exploration and expression of the seven directions." The explication is so brief for each piece that they can all be included here:

> 1. *Centering: The Dawn of Self awareness. Discovery. Hope and apprehensions. Finding one's center.*
> 2. *East. Sunrise. Creation. Beginning the quest. Spring. (see East Prayer).*
> 3. *South: Noon. Summer. Growth. Trust. The path of the adult Self.*
> 4. *West: The evening sky. Dusk. The transitions of light into darkness, life to death, and other major life changes. (see West Prayer).*
> 5. *North: Darkness. In the unpredictability of winter, Polaris maintains constancy. Reflection and reorganization.*
> 6. *Day Sky-Night Sky: The Heavens. The Father. Expansiveness and outward growth. The universe of possibilities.*
> 7. *Earth: The Mother. Fertility and bounty. Our bodies. Creating as well as destroying. There, here, and now. Home.*
> 8. *Within (Recentering): Re-membering. Returning to the Self.*

Finding that the seven cardinal directions always lead back to a place near the origin once removed, like a spiral. What exists within us also surrounds us.

The two prayers alluded to, above, are printed side by side in the notes:

East Prayer

I see you.
I see you, of light and warmth;
You Sun Bearer, White Shell Dawn;
Spotted Wind, White Corn, and as the
thunder in a young Eagle's mouth,
give life and growthful awareness
to all of us. As you serve us, know us
also and give to us that which you have
been charged with providing for us.

West Prayer

I carry within me the power of creation,
but those things over which I have no
control will enable me to see beyond my pitiful
self and become truly One with
all life here in my home. I will become
One with my power again and will see all
that I Am.
Ahu, Ahu.

We have created for ourselves a continually re-created world of dreams and experiences that are emulated in many traditions alike.

There are two statements by the two artists:

> *We have created for ourselves a continually re-created world of dreams and experiences that are emulated in many traditions alike. The voyage of discovery begins with defining one's point of being of "from where I now stand," and seeing the world from that perspective in a responsible and respectful manner.*
> —R. Carlos Nakai

> *I was born to a German family in Munich about 5,000 miles from Carlos' birthplace in America's Southwest. But when he and I walked into the studio and started to play, all the miles between us, all our traditional and cultural divisions, fell away. It seemed that through our music we started to re-member our common origin, our common ground. That we are all 'Natives' of the Earth.*
> —Peter Kater

Musically, Kater's piano occupies the position of prominence. It is characteristic of Nakai that in all his collaborations his impulse is to blend and submerge himself in the group rather than to dominate as a "star." There are times when the piano and flute do fit together as in "North," where the piano is murmuring in a low register. "East" and "West" include vocal chanting and whispering at the end of each piece. Perhaps these are the prayers mentioned above. The eagle-bone whistle is heard in "East" and "Day Sky." In the latter Nakai's flute again comes into its own, with the piano at a restrained minimum. "Earth" begins with Plains style singing to a rattle accompaniment. There is also a somewhat indistinct vocal part in a deep, electronicized voice. The eagle-bone whistle is important here, also.

Winter Dreams, 1990.

In this second album with William Eaton, Nakai realizes again his artistic and philosophical goal of mingling Native American culture, on equal terms, with cultures of other traditions through music. In the program notes, also, there is a search for common ground:

> *As a Diné (Navajo) R. Carlos Nakai's world has two seasons. Summer is the explosive recreation of the natural world balanced by the quiet of the winter season. This is the time to reassess personal experiences in the journey of life and to respect all that has been created for survival and enjoyment by the Yei, Coyote, and the First People. So too, in the Christian celebration of the birth of Christ, the darkest time of the year is the time of introspection, of renewal of hope and faith, of thanksgiving for the gifts of life. In this spirit, R. Carlos Nakai and guitarist William Eaton arranged these beautiful Christmas songs from Europe. It is as if these melodies carried themselves from the Old World across the New . . . to the Southwestern deserts where the wind and solitude imbued them with a new enchantment. . . .*

The two musicians take turn-about while playing the familiar carols together. After an improvisatory prelude, one carries the melody while the other provides an accompaniment of creative embellishments. Then they switch roles, all the while achieving an elegant blend of performance technique and musical imagination. In addition to the flute and the guitar, lyre, and harp guitar, there are long sustaining chords on the synthesizer, bird sounds, and other mild electronic effects. There is some use of soft percussion, the eagle-bone whistle, and echo effects. In the

last piece, "Silent Night," the carol is sung in Navajo by the Smith Family
Gospel Singers.

I will list the carols with parenthetical comments on effects that struck
me as especially interesting: Side A, band 1, "I Saw Three Ships"; band 2,
"What Child is This/Greensleeves" (here at one point, while the harp guitar
is carrying the melody, the flute holds a lovely descant note on the 5th, then
continues in a carefully organized counterpoint); band 3, "Angels We Have
Heard"; band 4, "We Three Kings"; band 5, "Lo, How a Rose Eer Blooming"
(this short rendition is by Eaton, alone). Side B, band 1, "God Rest Ye Merry
Gentlemen"; band 2, "The First Noel" (here the non-European tuning of
the flute stands out against the strings with an interestingly medieval
effect); band 3, "Coventry Carol" (flutter-tone on the flute, birdcalls, and
echoes make this a special production; it is the longest piece in the album);
band 4, "The First Snowfall" (by Eaton and Nakai, sounds entirely improvised; the steady flow of eighth notes gives a musical impression of falling
snow); band 5, "Silent Night" (the synthesizer guitar holds a long pulsating
chord on the tonic, over which the tune begins on high pinging notes on
the harp guitar. As the melody progresses the synthesizer guitar moves to
the dominant when appropriate. The Smith Family sings so softly that the
fact that the text is in Navajo only dawns on one gradually).

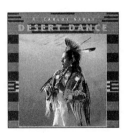

Desert Dance, 1990.

> *Desert Dance is my ritual about the ever-changing beauty of
> the San Luis Valley and the rain-laden sweep of clouds over Crestone
> and Lindisfarne in the late summer season of 1989. This improvisa-
> tional recording session, like* Sundance Season, *was hinted at in
> the beginning and became a personal reality as the days progressed
> . . . the San Luis Valley [is] the world's largest alpine valley at
> 8,000 feet above sea level, 100 miles long by 60 miles wide . . . [it]
> is sacred ground to the many tribes who have inhabited it over time,
> including the early pueblo dwellers, Athapascan nomads, Comanche,
> Kiowa, Arapahoe, Ute, and in the recent past the Spanish settlers,
> American explorers, and ranchers. Near Alamosa where the Great
> Sand Dunes lie, is the place of emergence for the Taos, the site of the
> Navajo's eastern sacred mountain, Blanca Peak, and the center of
> the Ute world.*

After this statement by Nakai, the album notes contain a long quotation
about the voices of landscapes from *Secrets from the Center of the World* by
Joy Harjo and Stephen Strom (Arizona Press, 1989), and a listing of four

other books on sacred places, the arts, and the spirituality of Native America.

The celebration of place has been noted above as an important motive in Nakai's work. This is his first album to focus on one place. Of the seventeen pieces, two are entirely vocal and five others intersperse voice with flute. This is also a new emphasis in Nakai's recordings. His voice has a Southern Plains quality and there are Plains-style drop-offs or glissandos at the ends of cadences. In the first piece, "Ancient Ground," Nakai's notes say that he is singing about the San Luis Valley "to all those who have come before." The notes for the all-vocal "Medicine Keeper" give a central message on Nakai's artistic perspective: "A vocalization about the unique beauty and self-defined inclusiveness within this sacred territory." For "Pollen Pathway": "Centering oneself in response to all life within my sacred and alive universe, where I now stand."

A powerful orientation to place and one's kinship with place has been stated all through Nakai's writings accompanying his music. "Inclusive" is one of his key words. The artist invites his listeners to join him on a religious and philosophical journey.

Though, as we have seen, this inclusiveness has led to a wide range of collaborative works, the present album is one of Nakai's solo performances. There is some experimentation with brushing and tapping a big drum, and tremolo and rhythmic use of a rawhide rattle accompanies the voice. All through the album the flute, sometimes alternating with the voice, has the quiet, contemplative spirituality" and "delicate, graceful style" that has won him so many listeners (Birchall 1989). Two pieces performed on the nose flute introduce a slightly more breathy sound.

In the notes, Nakai includes the dimension of time past, as well as place: *Land of Emergence, a nose flute solo, similar to the ones found in archaeological sites through the Anasazi Southwest.*

Atlantic Crossing, 1990.

This is Nakai's first overseas collaboration and was distributed privately only in Europe. This recording results from a European tour of eighteen concerts in 1988 with Paul and Limpe Fuchs. Paul Fuchs, like Eaton, has invented a number of unique musical instruments such as tubedrums, ballaststrings, bronzedrums, stoneblades, and the Fuchshorns. With Limpe, he has created a performing program called "Anima;" they met Nakai at the World Music Seminar and this led to the European tour.

Centering oneself
in response to
all life within my
sacred and alive
universe, where
I now stand.

The album begins with Nakai's quiet singing, accompanied by a rattle. The next cut is an instrumental ensemble, followed again by the solo voice. At the end of the first side we hear Nakai's flute for the first time. He also plays the eagle-bone whistle in ensemble with the "Anima" instruments. The second side begins with the Native American flute, solo, and has Nakai's flute, voice, and other instruments on the other two cuts. The recording was made at the Free Music Center in Munich, and the sound of the traffic outside can be heard, "replacing the wind and the rushing water in the canyons of Arizona." The Fuchs' instrumental music, throughout, is improvisatory and largely percussive, in free rhythms. According to the notes the goal is to represent the "age-old wisdom of humankind."

Spirit Horses, 1991.

Another kind of collaboration began for Nakai in 1986 when Canyon Records, his principal publisher, commissioned a concerto for chamber orchestra and Native American flute. It was stipulated that the work would incorporate some of the melodies that were played by Ed Lee Natay, the first Native American artist to be recorded by Canyon Records. The composer is James DeMars, a professor at Arizona State University, and the work, "Spirit Horses," was performed in 1986 in Scottsdale, Arizona, to celebrate the thirty-fifth anniversary of Natay's first record.

Nakai and DeMars collaborated on several more compositions: "Premonitions of Christopher Columbus" in 1987, "Colors Fall" and "Tapestry V" in 1988, and "Two World Symphony" in 1989. A second concerto for Nakai, to be written by DeMars, was commissioned by the Phoenix Symphony and premiered in 1993.

The album *Spirit Horses* contains the 1986–88 works listed above. It begins with "Premonitions of Christopher Columbus," which opens with Nakai's flute playing the "Zuni Sunrise Song" followed by sensitive orchestral elaborations on this theme. "Tapestry V" was inspired by a Baudelaire poem, and the melodies for the flute "feature ornamentation adapted from Navajo song style extended to emulate speech and bird song." "Colors Fall" is a duet for Native American flute and European flute: The primary melodic material was adapted from a 'Hopi Harvest Dance Song,' again taken from Natay's 1951 recording. "Spirit Horses" also begins with the "Zuni Sunrise Song" and draws its inspiration from Jerome Rothenberg's "reworking" of a Navajo Horse Song (Rothenberg 1969:302).

Migration, 1992.

Here Nakai joins forces again with Peter Kater, two years after *Natives*. Kater was the producer and wrote the notes, which make it clear that the album is a collaborative work and that Nakai is the chief collaborator:

> *I originally conceived of this album as a sort of map for creating and experiencing ritual in one's life . . . in the sense of conscious, formalized actions . . . R. Carlos and I sat down with Chris White and Hunt Harris(both people with active ritual lives) to further explore this concept and come up with our first outline.*

The twelve cuts have titles that seem to express both physical and spiritual migration: "Wandering," "Initiation," "Honoring," "Stating Intention,". . . "Becoming Human," "Walking the Path," and, finally, "Service: Transcendence of the Illusion of Separateness. Humility. Joy." The album opens with Kater's free-form piano under which we hear a spoken invocation by Nakai, in Navajo. Then comes a cello and, as the sections of the album progress, female voices, the eagle-bone whistle, Nakai's flute, a vocal chorus, synthesizer, soprano saxophone. Nakai as speaker, chanter, and instrumentalist is on every cut. The whole work is dreamy, quiet and, as the notes say, "delicate and spacious."

Ancestral Voices, 1992.

This recording is Nakai's third collaboration with guitarist William Eaton and, as mentioned before, was a Grammy Awards finalist in the category of "Best Traditional Folk Music." As in many of his previous recordings, this is a musical theater production, developing a consistent theme. It is in three parts: "Witnesses:" the dreams and daring of the European ancestors who ventured into the unknown, "First People:" an evocation of the Indigenes who were already here, and "Dreams:" an eventual union with the spirit of the newcomers.

The two musicians illustrate this story with various musical combinations: Nakai with Native American flute, eagle bone whistle, gourd rattle, shaker, claves, and voice; Eaton with harp guitar, koto harp guitar, o'ele'n strings, vihuela, synth guitar, bow harp, drums, 12 string guitar, and lyre. Many of these stringed instruments are Eaton's own inventions. In two of the episodes the Black Lodge Singers of White Swan, Washington, provide vocals.

As in the first Nakai-Eaton record, *Carry the Gift,* each of the 18 compositions has an explicatory poem. "Beyond the Edge" expresses the fear of early voyagers that they might fall off the edge of the world. "Stone Mirage" is inspired by the idea of a child pointing at petroglyphs of armored men searching for treasure; "Unfolding Sky" conveys the image of an old woman who has seen the worn trails of her youth become paved highways, but

> *Humans pass like clouds.*
> *Father sky is everywhere*
> *Embracing the precious struggle.*

In part two the natives begin to teach the newcomers how "to become as 'the people' and we see how they impart to the Europeans respect for the natural world, the harmony of a spiritual view of the world, the rebirth implicit in rain, the quiet power of Earth Mother.

In an introductory statement Nakai and Eaton speak of their work as ". . . part of the ageless cycle of the creation of new stories and traditions that belong to the personal experiences of all native Americans, regardless of their ancestry. . . ."

The music is a quiet blending of the Plains flute with Eaton's gentle strings. In six of the pieces we hear Nakai's singing, with vocables or perhaps words so soft we do not know the language. In the last piece, "Many Flags," in his persona as Two Crows, Nakai prays, and the pow-wow Flag Song by the Black Lodge Singers is an icon for the uniting of the two hemispheres.

Emergence: Songs of the Rainbow World, 1992.

This record is a return to the Nakai of the first album, *Changes*. Starting with traditional melodies from the North and Central Plains, adapted to the flute, the program goes on to celebrate "whirlwinds dancing and in the Sonoran desert," hawks, coyotes, and sunsets. "The Young Old Warrior" is dedicated to "young people sticking to old traditions." "Willow people" reaffirms Nakai's universalist perspective, "All life-forms here are of water and like the sacred willow celebrate by dancing in the winds."

The next four songs, under the heading, "Songs of the Rainbow World," ". . . are my musical interpretations of the Diné (Navajo) creation and emergence stories as performed in my concert program." They represent three underworlds, black, blue-green and yellow-white, which Nakai associates with the Amazon Basin, the evolution of water and sky, and the Andes and Central America. The fourth, Rainbow, world was ". . . given us by the Yeibichai (grandfathers of the gods) as a gift to be used responsibly and wisely." The recording ends with Nakai's encore piece, a rendition of "Amazing Grace," transmuted with echoes and grace-notes.

The album notes contain a concise history of the revival of the Native American flute, Nakai's part in this development, and comments on the flute's capabilities. The back cover presents a statement of his personal philosophy of music "built, like a new house on an old foundation., upon the ancient songs and stories sought from many traditions and sources."

The iconography of this album is the only one of the recent productions showing the artist in full Native outfit. We see the dazzling quillwork, "scalp-lock" fringes, deerhoof bandoleer, and beautifully tanned and painted buckskin that he wears in his concert performances.

How the West Was Lost, I, 1993.

Here Nakai returns to his collaboration with Peter Kater (*Natives, Migration*) but in still another new musical venture: the creation of a television soundtrack. This album contains 23 selections from a six-hour miniseries emphasizing that for the West to be won, somebody had to lose it. Nakai's flutes, chanting, rattles and eagle bone whistle are combined with Kater's piano, and with synthesizers and strings, woodwinds., percussion and vocals by 14 other musicians and a Native American pow-wow group, the White Oak Singers.

The selections range in length from a minute and a half to about four minutes; they tell the story of the defeat and pauperization of the Native Americans in the second half of the nineteenth century, ". . . a tribute to Native peoples everywhere and a prayer that their culture, traditions and rituals may persevere. . . ."

The titles, like a bell tolling betrayal and defeat: include "Dull Knife and Little Wolf," "Crazy Horse Prayer," "Last of the Buffalo," "Sand Creek Memories," "Nez Perce Flight Song," "Surrender," and "I Will Fight No More." Nakai composed "Crazy Horse Prayer," and "Last of the Buffalo," and, with Kater, composed "Navajo Land Blessing," "He Came from the Black Hills," and "I Will Fight No More." In most of these his chanting and sotto voce speaking are important components. A theme, beginning 1, 3b, 4, 5, 4 3b, 1, 1 appears throughout the work, giving it unity, as does the prevailingly minor mode.

The visual illustrations in the notes are old photographs of eloquent Native faces from the National Anthropological Archives. Each of these unsmiling faces is a reproach to the winners of the West.

Boat People, 1993.

In this year the ethnic jazz band, Jackalope, founded by Nakai in 1986, reappears in two new volumes. As in the earlier recordings, the theme of protest is carried by often bilingual, biting puns and other outbreaks of outrageous wit. This volume is by Nakai and his Hispanic collaborator, Larry Yañez. The former contributes Central, North and South American flutes, percussion, chanting, trumpet, shell horn, found objects and electronic re-processing; from the latter we hear keyboards, acoustic and electric guitar, guitar synthesizer, Oaxacan flutes, whistles, percussion and found objects.

The narrative, begun in the two earlier volumes, resumes with a prophet dog (Rasta' Perro) appearing to the Aztecs, predicting the arrival of strangers and great changes. Then follow the appearance of Vikings, the Spaniards and Buster Custer, "descendant of the con-quizi-neadors."

It ends at the Border with street chiefs joking about Christoph Hitler's birthday. All these boat people founder in a sea of "Synthacousticpunk-arachiNavajazz." Yañez' double entendre drawings, in the notes, add to the frolicking, ironic tone of the whole production.

Dances With Rabbits, 1993.

The fourth Jackalope serio-spoof adds the music of J. David Muñiz and Will Clipman to that of Nakai and Yañez. The array of musical instruments, acoustic and electric, is too formidable to list here in full, but includes the Jupiter B-flat pocket trumpet, TS10 tube screamer classic., Sequential Circuits IPS33B super harmony machine, djimbe drum, caxixis, and mesquite pod. In contrast to the dreamy, arhythmic quality of most of the Nakai oeuvre, the listener wants to dance all through the album: salsa, rock, waltz, tango and Native round dance.

The story goes on: Dog Soldier and Lord Fumamota return with two confederates., "Jeezus Munnies" and "Honest Ozzie;" we learn the viewpoint and follow the adventures of the four warriors. They bust in Tijuana, surf in the tsunami caused by the collapse of the ice bridge at Bering Strait, pray in the Sonoran desert, burn their fingers on hot sausages and imbibe endless cervesas. This gives us the title of cut # 10: "Und Zen Zer Vas," in which Nakai's chanting is a prayer song to Jackalope and also "the fight song of Shaman U." The album ends with "Fried Bread Grease Blues," in which Dog Soldier and Lord Fumamota "reminisce about the pall of choking vapors wafting through an improperly ventilated indoor fine arts show. Or where there's smoke there's a fire sale."

The philosophy, a restorative after the pain of *How the West was Lost* is to enjoy ourselves by laughing off ancient injustices and cutting down to size the old pretensions that separate us from one another.

Native Tapestry, 1994.

This album is almost the opposite of the preceding one in that it represents Nakai's fullest excursion into the new world of orchestral art music in specially commissioned works by the Arizona composer, James DeMars. It continues the collaboration that began with *Spirit Horses* in 1991. The first three pieces, "Crow Wing," "Lake That Speaks," and "Spirit Call," are derived, from DeMars' "Two World Concerto (for Native American Flute and Orchestra)."

They begin with a tranquil duet with flute and saxophone, go on with cello, vibraphone and piano, and reach a peak of intensity with the addition of the djimbe, a "talking" drum from West Africa.

The rest of the record contains DeMars' "Two World Symphony," a work that was commissioned by the Arizona Committee on the French Revolution. The commission stipulated the inclusion of the Native American flute, African percussion, strings, woodwinds, and French poetry. The latter is by Michel Sarda, declaimed by the author, and evokes the American Southwest. The symphony is an expression of the growing trend towards world music performances. The cellist, Xiaozhong Zheng, is a native of China who studied cello performance there and at Arizona State University; one of the percussionists, Mark Sunkett, is an ethnomusicologist from Philadelphia who has studied with master musicians in a number of West African cultures. All these talents, and musical and literary elements are brought together in a work of impressive force and clarity.

Island of Bows, 1994.

Like *Atlantic Crossing,* this album is an example of Nakai's gift for collaboration, carried to international lengths, this time in Japan. Here he combines with the Wind Travelin' Band from the Kansai area; six musicians who play traditional instruments from Asia and Africa. In the album they perform with koto, erhu, shakuhachi, yan-chin, kalimba, shamisen, percussion and voice. In addition, Shonosuke Ohkura plays the otsuzumi, and Oki Kano, a descendant of the Ainu people in Hokkaido, plays the tonkori, a mountain dulcimer-like instrument from his tribal tradition.

The music features the plangent, nasal sound of the erhu, duets by the Native American flute and the shakuhachi which has a similar, hauntingly mellow sound, and the sharp "pow" of the otsuzumi drum as it is heard in Noh drama. Much of the record is dreamy flute music accompanied by gentle strings. Echoes and simulated bird cries give a forest ambiance to the whole production. Titles of the seven pieces underscore this motif: "Sunrise," "Island of Bows," (in Japanese myths the islands are thought to form a curve in the shape of a bow), "KAMUI," (in Ainu this means "good," "the highest," "God."), "Cloud Temple," "Night Forest," "Red Wind." The recording was made in the Hounji Temple in Kyoto.

Nakai and Wind Travelin' Band both have, in the notes, statements of purpose which show the unity of their philosophy of art and life. Nakai: ". . . our uniquely personal oral traditions encourage sharing and understanding the commonality of our journey to the Morning Star." Wind Travelin' Band: ". . . Humanity, the power to create what is genuine . . . growing aware of life's coexistence in the dawning era. . . ."

Honorable Sky, 1994.

This collaboration with Peter Kater joins with David Darling (cello), Paul McCandless (oboe, penny whistle), and Mark Miller (soprano saxophone) on an "improvisational journey, exploring male soulfulness and intimacy in our world today." A statement by Kater avers that Mother Earth needs a worthy masculine companion, open, strong, flexible and intuitive. Nakai's philosophy, 'underlying the project, is that males need to learn to express their vulnerability and "unconditional LOVE, first for oneself, then for the surrounding environment of life in its various manifestations."

The prevailing musical expression of these feelings is by Kater's wide arpeggiations on the piano supporting the other instruments as they take turns improvising. Occasionally, all join together floating in a peaceful awareness of each other. Soulfulness appears in some of the titles, which taken all together create a litany of quiet introspection: "Gathering of Souls," "My Soul's Story," "If Men Were At Peace," "Honorable Sky.," "All Souls Waltz," "Essence," and "One Voice."

Nakai's statement is consistent with all his work. He goes beyond male soulfulness to embrace life in all its forms. "Honorable Sky" seems to derive from the Sky Father, counterpart of Earth Mother in Navajo thought, and that of many other cultures around the world.

The album cover is a painting of five male figures by Lindsey Leavell, entitled "Honor." They are standing in the desert in campesino costume, heads bowed, hands in pockets, deep in introspection.

How the West Was Lost, II, 1995.

This recording is made up of further selections from the sound track composed by Peter Kater for a television mini-series. The notes contain the same homage to Native Peoples everywhere as in the first record of this title. Here, however, the musical selections make references to eastern as well as western Indian tribes.

Nakai collaborated with Kater in the composition of "Hand in Hand," "White River Utes," "Challenge at White River,' "Chief Ouray's Death Song," and "Grandmother's Lament." Joanne Shenandoah, another Canyon Records artist, performed and organized the sound in "Iroquois Longhouse," and "Dance of the North" which are listed as "Haudeenosaunee-Iroquois chants in the public domain." Other eastern references are "Themes for the Cherokee," "The Seminole Everglades," "Cherokee Faith," and "Everglade Farewell."

Again there are twenty-four selections, brief and poignant., in minor modes and slow, improvisatory tempi. The White Oak Singers are heard, as before and there are additional "native chanting, hoots, and war cries," by Marty Goodbear.

As in *How the West Was Lost, I,* the notes are illustrated by unsmiling Native faces from the national Anthropological Archives. The two records show different faces but all underscore the message of defeat, loss, and departure carried by the song titles.

Feather, Stone and Light, 1995.

The most recent album to date is Nakai's fourth collaboration with William Eaton and includes percussionist Will Clipman who has also played with Jackalope. His interest in "worldbeat polyrhythms" adds many of the following instruments to the ensemble: tom-toms, udu, shekere, Cameroon bell, zils, djimbe, doumbek, bamboo mouth harp, Gila River powwow drum, nose flute, didjeridu, anklung, Bois d'arc sticks, Taos drum, tables and tingklik. The opening and closing sound on the record is thunder, the ultimate percussion.

Billed on the back of the album as a "trialogue...rooted in the Sonoran desert and colored by sounds of the whole world," these 18 group improvisations are built around ideas of a world united in dreams, nature, and the mystery of life. Representative titles are "Dreaming the World," "Savannah Sojourn," "The Lake Inside the Flower," "Sonoran Raga," "Midnight in the Sacred Grove" (an echo of "Nemi" in Earth Spirit, 1987), "Last Wild River."

Of all the eclectic variety of sound combinations, one of the most successful is a deep, strong synthesizer accompanying a pulsating didjeridu, an Australian aboriginal trumpet made of a hollow branch. Of course much of the sound in the album as a whole is the mix of Eaton's harp guitar and other strings with Nakai's haunting flute. Much of the music is dance music: the irresistible rhythms of Will Clipman add this joyous element to the program, as in *Dances with Rabbits*.

2

THE QUESTION OF AUTHENTICITY

ESPITE FERVENT EFFORTS
TO LAY IT TO REST, THE NOTION OF "AUTHENTICITY" LOOMS
PERSISTENTLY IN ANTHROPOLOGICAL (Joralemon, 1990:105–18)
and ethnomusicological discourse. In considering the question, I will start
with how we define our field. Jaap Kunst delimited it, in the first book with
"ethnomusicology" in the title, as being concerned with certain geographical
and cultural "non-" areas: principally non-European, non-art musics (1955:9).
Mieczyslaw Kolinski's rejoinder held that the field is defined by its method,
rather than by the regions studied or not studied (1957). Bruno Nettl's most
recent overview of the field shows that, in fact, nearly all of us, whatever
our method, do delimit our subject in the way Kunst observed, thirty-five
years ago (1983:4).

If we are, indeed, scholars of a particular range of musical genres in
specified parts of the world, it follows that we define by our work what
these genres are. By identifying styles (ibid., 118–27) we also certify them,

whether that is our intention or not. When I recorded a Penobscot singer fifty years ago, he referred me to a transcription of the song as he had performed it for Frank Speck, published in *Penobscot Man* (1940) to see "if I've got it right."

Alan Lomax feels that a particular music fits the common ethos of its performers with such psychic power that if they lose the music they will fall into a kind of anomie he calls "cultural greyout" (1968:4–6). He sees, all about us, dying cultures becoming musically inauthentic and calls on ethnomusicologists and folklorists to find ways to save these endangered species (1977, 1989). He was a major force leading to the enactment of the American Folklife Preservation Act by the United States Congress in 1976 and the founding of the American Folklife Center at the Library of Congress (Kurin 1989:16). There can be problems, however, in deciding just which genres and cultural life-styles should be preserved.

In my own study of the music of "Native Americans" I have also found it hard, sometimes, to identify what this term means.

In my own study of the music of "Native Americans" I have also found it hard, sometimes, to identify what this term means. It was coined to rectify Columbus's misapprehension as to what and whom he "discovered" in 1492. But if we mean by "natives," people of aboriginal ancestry in United States territory, we have to include Polynesians and Inuits. In the never-ending grand mixture of cultures and genres, when does the term "native" begin or cease to apply? The taxonomic quandary grows more perplexing with the passage of time.

The aboriginal people, whoever they are, have been involved in a flux of development from within, and influences from without, for 30,000 years since the first of many small groups of Asian immigrants crossed the Bering Straits into the New World. This process of cultures inventing and reinventing themselves began to incorporate ideas from Europe with the first Viking contacts a thousand years ago. Since then, influences from Africa and the rest of the world have added to the mix, as have biological traits in the genetic pool we call America.

In continental North America, the early Asian immigrants influenced each other for so many millennia that a culture-blend came into existence and was described by outsiders in the late nineteenth and early twentieth centuries as having certain general traits in common. Political organization, economy, and the arts were somewhat alike from ocean to ocean. The music, though differing in details, was mostly vocal and monophonic. It was largely religious and was designed to help in maintaining harmony with the forces of nature. Musical instruments were principally drums, rattles, and rasps to accompany the voice, but there were also flutes, flageolettes, and whistles. The isolation of North American native communities on reservations, starting in the eighteenth century and essentially accomplished by the mid-nineteenth century, preserved some of these cultural features for a few decades, though reservation life obviously made drastic changes in the form and meaning of the way people lived. On some reservations, music has been one of the holdovers from the pre-reservation period of Native American history, but Euro-American military bands, school bands, and Christian hymnody had a wide impact, as did popular musics of the dominant culture.

In the never-ending grand mixture of cultures and genres, when does the term "native" begin or cease to apply?

Much of our stereotype of the "authentic" (meaning pre-reservation) Native American includes European elements such as horses, guns, steel knives, tomahawks, brightly colored cloth, and glass beads. Where do we decide, in the cultural continuum, on the moment when Native American culture is still "authentic?"

In the case of music, there are today numerous new forms performed by the descendants of the early Asian immigrants. If these resemble some kind of popular or art music from the Euro-American repertory, how do we define them? I take my cue from Gen'ichi Tsuge, who used to start his course in Japanese music at Wesleyan University with a recording of a Beethoven Symphony. He would then inform his students that it was being performed by one of Tokyo's seven symphony orchestras and that it had been Japanese music for over one hundred years. In this spirit I consider that any music by any composer or performer who has anything to do with Native American culture, past or present, has to be recognized as some part of Native American music and is an "authentic" aspect of it in that moment of history in which it exists.

Some scholars with whom I have discussed Nakai's music have questioned whether it is "Indian" at all. There are Native Americans who describe much of the new Indian music as "Anglo music, performed/composed by Indians" (Isaacs 1988). Nakai has stated that Navajo traditionalists "Don't like my work, and say it's not Navajo" (Nakai 1991). He points out that the flute itself is not a Navajo instrument and may have been lost in the migration from Alaska to the Southwest (Means 1985).

Nakai's use of synthesizers and ethnic or newly created accompanying instruments from around the world and his collaboration with jazz and avant garde musicians here and abroad, in fact even his success with the non-Indian world audience, could all be said to be not-Indian. His excursions into the musicology of the Plains flute and his impressive collection of instruments are in the mode of the Euro-American scholar and collector. In many ways his career has been unlike that of any other Native American musician, yet his career and his work are also quintessentially Indian.

My definition of "authentic" Native American music is broad enough to obviate any reason for this paper if all I wanted to do was claim some "authenticity" for Nakai's work. Instead, I intended to describe the work for its own interest and explore the intricate web of its involvement in world culture, including Native American culture in the broad sense, and Navajo culture specifically.

To get rid of a principal bugaboo at once, Nakai's willingness to try anything, to mingle his creative output with elements of other musics, is very "Indian." Native American philosophy is "inclusive," as stated above; this is one of Nakai's key words. This receptivity to new ideas is also characteristic of East Asia in contrast to the exclusiveness of West Asia, Europe, and mainstream America, not counting its liberal, New Age, and other non-conforming populations. As I mentioned earlier, the Native people of America adopted whatever was brought to these shores by the more recent migrants, including the teachings of the many missionaries who came along. There are churches of every Christian sect on the reservations, but also a nationwide representation of the Native American Church, which had its nineteenth-century origins among the Paiutes of Nevada. There are thought to be 60,000 members of this church among the Navajos alone. The Plains Sundance is now having a revival all through the Western states and is being performed in new communities, including that of the Navajos. The inclusiveness of the new Native religions is one of their strongest appeals, and the exclusiveness of the Christian sects is often ignored by their Native members. Inclusiveness is one of Nakai's major teachings, implicit in the style of his music and explicit in his interviews: "I do want your children to become us. You are no longer Europeans, you are us now. . . . It is time for you to start learning how to be in our land" (Tayac 1989:40). Nakai, himself, is an icon of inclusiveness: a Navajo with Ute heritage whose surname means "Mexican," the name of whose mother's clan means "Zuni." On 4–5 March 1993 he played a Plains flute for the world premiere of the "Two World Concerto," by James DeMars, with the Phoenix Symphony.

In her chapter "Culture and Aesthetics" in *Native American Music,* Marcia Herndon contrasts the ego-centered emphasis of the West with the community-centered perspective of Native North America (1980:56–90).

Where do we decide, in the cultural continuum, on the moment when Native American culture is still "authentic?"

Nakai's long history of collaboration with other artists is a case in point; despite his popular success, the "star syndrome" is conspicuously absent from his performance, his commentaries, and his life style. In one of his interviews he said "We're a very socially oriented tribe. So everything we do can't be done as an individual" (Means 1985). After all, eighteen of the twenty five albums considered here are collaborative.

Nakai's keen interest in his Native American heritage is everywhere in his work. He draws inspiration from mountains, valleys, canyons, wind, rain, sunsets, the scent of juniper, from wild life, and from the earth itself. His music describes the Southwest particularly, and he has a vivid sense of his ancestors moving through this landscape. Anasazi ruins, immigration routes, and intertribal cultural influences have an important place in the liner notes.

The key word in Navajo religious philosophy is "hózhóó," "place, blessed" (or peaceful, harmonious, pleasing, beautiful). "Place" refers to any particular place, the total environment, the universe itself (Witherspoon 1977:23–40). Nakai's celebration of place occurs on many levels. One whole album celebrates the Colorado Rockies (*Sundance Season*), as stated above; another (*Desert Dance*) is dedicated to the San Luis Valley, "the largest Alpine valley in the world," and the people who have lived there from pre-historic times to the present. *Canyon Trilogy* is of a "mythic dreamscape"; *Natives* bears the universalist message that we are all "natives" of the earth. Nakai teaches not just the environmentalists' respect for nature but the Native American identification with it. In *Sundance Season*, five of the ten pages of notes are on the great earth renewal ceremony of the Plains, the Sundance. Nakai's teaching is religious, preaching awareness of the vital energy of the earth, essential for the spiritual journey of the individual. In the later albums, prayers, invocations, and chanting are heard interspersed with the music. When I asked him about this he said "I began putting in my voice as soon as I thought I could get away with it" (Nakai 1989).

I see a kinship between the clowning in the Jackalope recordings and the sacred clowns who have an important place in the ceremonials of the Pueblo and Navajo communities. They teach by burlesque and the potent vehicle of humor. The strong music-theater (ritual) element is evident in Nakai's public performances and also in the organization of his albums, in which the whole program is often devoted to the development of a single, complex theme.

The idea that Native American life and ideas contain powerful lessons for the rest of the world has been noted by other observers, as well as Nakai.

Nakai's keen interest in his Native American heritage is everywhere in his work. He draws inspiration from mountains, valleys, canyons, wind, rain, sunsets, the scent of juniper, from wild life, and from the earth itself.

The Pilgrim Fathers feared that the attractions of the Native American communities would lure young people away from Puritan theocratic control through what they called "Indianization" (Slotkin 1973:57–145). In *Winter Dreams* the European Christmas, itself, is Indianized by the winter sun in the Southwestern canyons, the statement of Navajo solstitial ideas, and the Native American flute playing its part in the variations and evocations of Christmas carols. The brilliant lawyer Felix Cohen wrote in "Americanizing the White Man" of the many ways in which Native Americans have, indeed, transformed European culture (Cohen 1951–52:177–91). Thomas Berry considers the Native American view of the mutuality between humankind and the land to be our greatest hope in reversing the degradation of the environment (1988:180–93).

Perhaps Nakai's musical and poetic statements of respect for the environment and the importance of a sense of kinship with the natural world will give these insights their widest hearing. His international audience is listening.

REFERENCES

Ballard, Louis W.
    1973 *American Indian Music for the Classroom: Teacher's Guide.* Phoenix, Ariz.: Canyon Records.
Berry, Thomas
    1988 *The Dream of the Earth.* San Francisco: Sierra Club Books.
Birchall, Steve
    1989 Review of "Carry the Gift" and "Earth Spirit." *Audio* 73, no. 12.
Boardman, Eunice, and Beth Landis
    1966 *Exploring Music 5.* New York: Holt, Rinehart and Winston.
Caputo, Salvatore
    1988 "Flutist Puts Roots to Use in the'80's." *Arizona Republic* (Phoenix), November 9.
Cohen, Felix
    1951–52 "Americanizing the White Man." *American Scholar* 21:171–91.
Harjo, Joy, and Stephen Strom
    1989 *Secrets from the Center of the World.* Tucson: University of Arizona Press.
Herndon, Marcia
    1980 *Native American Music.* Norwood, Pa.: Norwood Editions.
Issacs, Tony
    1988 Personal communication.

Joralemon, Donald

1990 "The Kolinsk Selling of the Shaman and the Problem of Informant Legitimacy." *Journal of Anthropological Research* 46, no. 2:105–18.

Kisselgoff, Anna

1988 "Graham's New Look at the American Indian." *New York Times,* Arts/Entertainment section, October 15.

Kolinski, Mieczyslaw

1957 "Ethnomusicology, Its Problems and Methods." *Ethnomusicology Newsletter 10:1–7.*

Kunst, Jaap

1955 *Ethnomusicology.* The Hague, Netherlands: Martinus Nijoff.

Kurin, Richard

1989 "Why We Do the Festival." *1989 Festival of American Folklife,8–21.* Washington, D.C.: Smithsonian Institution.

Lomax, Alan

1968 *Folk Song Style and Culture.* Washington, D.C.: American Association for the Advancement of Science, Publication no. 88.

1977 "An Appeal for Cultural Equity." *Journal of Communication* 27 (spring): 125–38.

1989 Personal communication addressed to the business meeting of the Society for Ethnomusicology, November 11, Cambridge, Mass.

McAllester, David P.

1981–82 "New Perspectives in Native American Music." *Perspectives* of *New Music 20,* nos. 1–2:433–46.

1995 "The Music of R. Carlos Nakai," in From the Four Corners, Essays in Honor of Rose Brandel, ed., Ellen Leichtman, Harmonie Park Press, Warren, Michigan, pp. 189–210.

McAllester, David P., and Douglas F. Mitchell

1983 "Navajo Music." In *Handbook of North American Indians, vol. 10: Southwest,* 605–23. Washington, D.C.: Smithsonian Institution.

Means, Andrew

1985 "New Ground, Navajo Flutist Adds Measure to Tribe's Musical Traditions." *Arizona Republic* (Phoenix). Leisure and Arts section, June 6.

Nakai, R. Carlos

1989 Personal communication.

1991 Personal communication.

Nettl, Bruno

1983 *The* Study *of Ethnomusicology.* Urbana: University of Illinois Press.

Payne, Richard

1990 Personal communication.

Rothenberg, Jerome

1969 "America: A Prophecy." *Stony Brook 3/4.*

Slotkin, Richard

1973 *Regeneration Through* Violence. Middletown, Conn.: Wesleyan University Press.

Smythe, Willie

1989 "Songs of Indian Territory." *In Songs of Indian Territory: Native American Music Traditions of Oklahoma,* 67–69. Oklahoma City: Center of the American Indian.

Speck, Frank

1940 *Penobscot Man.* Philadelphia: University of Pennsylvania Press. Reprint, New York, Octagon Books, 1970.

Tayac, Gabrielle

1989 "Living in Two Worlds: R. Carlos Nakai, Ute/Navajo Flutist." *Northeast Indiana Quarterly* 6, no. 3 (fall): 38–41.

Troyer, Carlos

1913 *The Zuni Indians and Their Music.* Philadelphia: Theodore Presser Company.

Wheelwright, Mary C., ed. by David P. McAllester

1952 *Navajo Creation Chants. Song* 15. Cambridge: Peabody Museum.

Witherspoon, Gary

1977 *Language and Art in the Navajo Universe.* Ann Arbor: University of Michigan Press.

ACKNOWLEDGMENTS

I am grateful to R. Carlos Nakai for his generous responses to many queries, to Joan Quinn for information on the Zuni Sunrise song in various music readers, to Robert Doyle for much information on Canyon Records' role in the career of R. Carlos Nakai, to Ellen C. Leichtman for her extensive and helpful editorial suggestions and to Harmonie Park Press for their generous permission to use (with updating) my article in McAllester, 1995.

BIBLIOGRAPHY & DISCOGRAPHY

Bibliography

Adler, Samuel, *Eastman School of Music*, W.W. Norton and Co., New York, NY, 1982.

Bate, Philip, "The Flute," *Instruments of the Orchestra*, Benn & Norton, New York, NY, 1969.

Bowra, C.M., *Primitive Song*, The World Publishing Co., Cleveland, OH, 1962.

Clifford, James, *The Predicament of Culture*, Harvard University Press, Cambridge, MA, 1988.

Densmore, Frances, "The Study of Indian Music," *Smithsonian Report*, 1941, Facsimile reproduction, The Shorey Bookstore, Seattle, WA, 1966.

Fletcher, Neville H. and Suzanne Thwaites, "The Physics of Pipe Organ Pipes," pp 94-103, *Scientific American*, January, 1983.

Hensley, Betty Austin, "Love and Legend Speak, Some Native American Flutes," pp 14-21, *The Flutists Quarterly*, Winter 1985, The National Flute Association, Royal Oak, MI.

Kujala, Walfrid, *The Flutist's Progress*, Progress Press, Evanston, IL, 1970.

Light, Ken, "The Renaissance of the Native American Flute," *The Woodwind Quarterly*, Fall 1993.

McAllister, David P., *Handbook of North American Indians*, vol. 10, Smithsonian Institution, Washington, DC, 1983.

Pares, Gabriel, Harvey S. Whistler, ed., "Pares Scales for Flute or Piccolo, for individual study and like-instrument class instruction," Rubank, Inc., Miami, FL, 1964.

Payne, Richard W., The Plains Flute, pp 11-14, *The Flutists Quarterly*, vol. XIII, no. 4, Fall 1988, The National Flute Association, Inc., Ann Arbor, MI.

Pearce, Roy Harvey, *Savagism and Civilization*, The Johns Hopkins Press, Baltimore, MD, (1953), 1967.

Petersen, A.C., *Rubank Elementary Method*, Rubank Educational Library no. 38, "Flute or Piccolo, A fundamental course for individual or like-instrument class instruction," Rubank, Inc., Miami, FL, 1984.

Pierce, John R., *The Science of Musical Sound*, Scientific American Books, Inc., New York, NY, 1983.

Powers, William K., "The Art of Courtship Among the Oglala," *American Indian Art*, Spring, 1980, Vol. 5, No. 2, pp 40-47, Scottsdale, AZ.

Reed, H. Owen and Robert G. Sidnell, "The Materials of Music Composition," *Book I: Fundamentals*, Michigan State University, Addison-Wesley Publishing Co., Reading, MA, 1978.

Thomas, Robert K., *Community and Institution Among American Indian Groups*, Wayne State University, Detroit, MI.

Discography

Locke, Kevin, *Lakota Love Songs and Stories*, FS 4001-C, Feather Stone Records. Lakota Wiikiyo Olowan, Kevin Locke Productions.

Nevaquaya, Doc Tate, *Comanche Flute Music*, FE 4328, Ethnic Folkways Records.

Ware, Tom Mauchahty, *Flute Songs of the Kiowa and Comanche*, IH 2512, Indian House Music.

The Traditional and Contemporary Indian Flute, IS 5050, Indian Sounds Records.

ABOUT THE AUTHORS

R. Carlos Nakai

Of Navajo-Ute heritage, R. Carlos Nakai is the world's premiere performer of the Native American flute. Originally trained in classical trumpet and music theory by Ronald K. Bowen and Birley R. Gardner, Nakai was given a traditional cedar wood flute as a gift and challenged to see what he could do with it. His first album, *Changes,* was released on the Canyon Records label in 1983 and since then he has released over sixteen more recordings with Canyon. He has also recorded for Silverwave Records and Celestial Harmonies. He has contributed music for the Columbia Pictures version of *Geronimo,* the TNT series, *How the West Was Lost* and has scored music for the IMAX production, *Zion.* The great American choreographer, Martha Graham, used music from *Cycles* for one of her last dance works, "Night Chant."

Nakai has performed throughout the world leading the renaissance of the Native American flute by bringing the haunting, timeless sound of the traditional cedar flute to new listeners and into new musical styles. In addition to his solo appearances in the United States, Canada, Europe and Japan, Nakai has worked with guitarist William Eaton, pianist Peter Kater and founded the ethnic jazz ensemble, Jackalope. Nakai has worked with such diverse musical forces as the Wind Travelin' Band, a traditional Japanese group, and has performed as a member of Tos, a classical ensemble led by James DeMars. He has performed before sold out audiences with the Phoenix Symphony, Tucson Symphony, San Juan Symphony, California Symphony and the Saskatoon Symphony.

In 1992, Nakai received one of the highest awards the state of Arizona can bestow, the Governor's Art Award. In 1994 he was a Grammy finalist for his *Ancestral Voices* album with William Eaton and was awarded an honorary doctorate from Northern Arizona University. In 1995 the First Americans in the Arts gave him their first award for musical achievement for his career of performance, composition and education.

Nakai has earned a Master's Degree in American Indian Studies from the University of Arizona. Nakai sees his role as a performer of the traditional flute not to reiterate the traditional sounds but to find new avenues of expression for the cultures of native peoples.

James DeMars

Of French-Canadian heritage, James DeMars earned his doctorate in music composition at the University of Minnesota where he studied with Dominick Argento, Eric Stokes and Donald Betts. In 1981, he began teaching at Arizona State University and organized the Tos Ensemble. DeMars has composed several cantatas including *The Prophet* (based on the writings of the Sufi teacher Rumi) which received its New York debut at Carnegie Hall. His works have been performed regularly by the Phoenix Symphony including the *Two World Overture* and *Two World Concerto (for Native American Flute and Orchestra)*. His first recording, *Spirit Horses,* featuring R. Carlos Nakai, was selected by *Pulse!* magazine as one of the best recordings of 1991. In 1995 his *American Requiem* was performed by the Mormon Tabernacle Choir at the Kennedy Center in Washington, D.C. and St. John the Divine Cathedral in New York. In May 1996, the Phoenix Symphony premiered *Native Drumming,* a concerto for symphony and pow-wow drum group which featured the Black Lodge Singers.

David P. McAllester

One of America's eminent music scholars, David P. McAllester was born in Massachusetts in 1916. He earned his B.A. from Harvard in 1938 and his Ph.D. from Columbia University in 1949. In 1947 he began teaching at Wesleyan where he founded the anthropology department and ethnomusicology program. He retired from Wesleyan in 1986.

McAllester was one of the four founders of the Society for Ethnomusicology in 1952. He has been a fellow of the American Anthropological Association, American Academy of Arts and Sciences, Guggenheim Foundation, Carnegie Foundation, National Science Foundation, Fulbright Program and Tokyo National Research Institute of Cultural Properties. He has served as a visiting professor at the University of Hawaii, Yale University, Academy of Gamelan Arts (Surakarta, Java), University of Sydney (Australia), Queensland University (Australia), Brown University, Smith College and Williams College.

McAllester's field research in Native American music, religious literature and ceremonialism has included the Hopi, Navajo, Penobscot, Passmaquoddie, Apache, Zuni, Comanche, Laguna and Menomini peoples. His major publications are *Peyote Music* (1949), *Enemy Way Music* (1954), *Myths and Prayers of the Great Star Chant* (ed., 1956), *Navajo Blessingway Singer* (co-editor with Charlotte Frisbie, 1978), *Hogans, Navajo Houses and Songs* (co-author with Susan W. McAllester, 1980), *Worlds of Music* (co-author with Jeff Titon, editor, et al, 1983) and *Becoming Human Through Music: The Wesleyan Symposium on the Perspectives of Social Anthropology in the Teachings and Learning of Music* (organizer and editor). He has over eighty articles, three recordings and one film to his credit.

Ken Light

A former science teacher, Light made his first Native American flute in 1985 using a design based on a 125-year-old Lakota courting flute loaned by his friend, Tony Shearer. Light first sold his flutes at local art fairs throughout Montana and the Pacific Northwest and via mail order. In 1987 he met R. Carlos Nakai at a flute festival in Colorado and began crafting flutes for Nakai's use. Soon, the flutist and instrument maker began working together to develop new configurations for the traditional flute. They began to conduct annual summer workshops called, "The Renaissance of the Native American Flute," at a ranch in Montana and later added a second winter workshop in Arizona. Light has crafted over 1,600 flutes and is recognized as one of the leading instrument makers in the world, crafting flutes under the Amon Olorin name.